T0224568

Ensemble Learning for AI Developers

Learn Bagging, Stacking, and Boosting Methods with Use Cases

Alok Kumar
Mayank Jain

Apress®

Ensemble Learning for AI Developers

Alok Kumar
Gurugram, India

Mayank Jain
Gurugram, India

ISBN-13 (pbk): 978-1-4842-5939-9
https://doi.org/10.1007/978-1-4842-5940-5

ISBN-13 (electronic): 978-1-4842-5940-5

Managing Director, Apress Media LLC: Welmoed Spahr
Acquisitions Editor: Celestin Suresh John
Development Editor: Laura Berendson
Coordinating Editor: Aditee Mirashi

Cover designed by eStudioCalamar

Cover image designed by Freepik (www.freepik.com)

Distributed to the book trade worldwide by Springer Science+Business Media New York, 233 Spring Street, 6th Floor, New York, NY 10013. Phone 1-800-SPRINGER, fax (201) 348-4505, e-mail orders-ny@springer-sbm.com, or visit www.springeronline.com. Apress Media, LLC is a California LLC and the sole member (owner) is Springer Science + Business Media Finance Inc (SSBM Finance Inc). SSBM Finance Inc is a **Delaware** corporation.

For information on translations, please e-mail rights@apress.com, or visit http://www.apress.com/rights-permissions.

Apress titles may be purchased in bulk for academic, corporate, or promotional use. eBook versions and licenses are also available for most titles. For more information, reference our Print and eBook Bulk Sales web page at http://www.apress.com/bulk-sales.

Any source code or other supplementary material referenced by the author in this book is available to readers on GitHub via the book's product page, located at https://www.apress.com/us/book/978-1-4842-5939-9. For more detailed information, please visit http://www.apress.com/source-code.

Printed on acid-free paper

This book is dedicated to my family for their unfettered support.

—Alok Kumar

To my family and Anand Sir, who unbounded my mind.

—Mayank Jain

Table of Contents

About the Authors

Alok Kumar is an AI practitioner and Innovation Lead at Publicis Sapient. He has extensive experience in leading strategic initiatives and driving cutting-edge, fast-paced innovations. His work has won several awards. Alok is passionate about democratizing AI knowledge. He manages multiple nonprofit learning and creative groups in National capital region of India NCR. Find him on LinkedIn at https://in.linkedin.com/in/aloksaan.

Mayank Jain is a technology manager and AI/ML expert at the Publicis Sapient Kepler Innovation Lab. He has more than 10 years of experience working on cutting-edge projects that involve making computers see and think by using techniques like deep learning, machine learning, and computer vision. He has written for several international publications, he has several patents in his name, and has been awarded multiple times for his contributions. Find him on LinkedIn at https://in.linkedin.com/in/mayankjain7.

About the Technical Reviewer

Ashutosh Parida is the head of analytics at Manipal Global Education Services in Bangalore. He has a decade of experience in data science, including vision, natural-language understanding, recommendation engines, and forecasting. He has been site lead for multiple projects and has launched products that serve millions of users. He also has open source contributions to his credit.

Ashutosh has a bachelor's degree in computers science and engineering from IIIT-Hyderabad. He has been in the IT industry for 15 years, having worked with Oracle, Samsung, Akamai, and Qualcomm. Find him on LinkedIn at https://www.linkedin.com/in/ashutoshparida/.

Acknowledgments

We would really like to thank the team at Apress for all their help and support in our journey writing this book. It has been a pleasure to write this book, and the team at Apress are certainly a big part of that. Many thanks to Acquisitions Editor, Celestin Suresh John, who was a great help in narrowing the scope of this project and making it more accessible. Many thanks to our development coordinators and our editors, Aditee Mirashi and Laura C. Berendson. Their continuous follow-up helped us tremendously with keeping us on track and focused. We are also thankful to Ashutosh Parida for his valuable technical feedback.

As always, we would like to thank our family for all their help and support. Without their support and assistance, we couldn't have completed this book.

Lastly, we would like to thank the open source community, who has helped democratize the knowledge. All the libraries used in this book come from open source projects.

Introduction

Ensemble learning is fast becoming a popular choice for machine learning models in the data science world. Ensemble methods combine the output of machine learning models in many interesting ways. Even after years of working on machine learning projects, we were unaware of the power of ensemble methods, as this topic is usually neglected or only given a brief overview in most machine learning courses and books. Like many others, we came to know about the power of ensemble methods by checking competitive machine learning scenarios. Competitive machine learning platforms, like Kaggle, offer an unbiased review of machine learning techniques. For the past few years, ensemble learning methods have consistently outperformed competitive metrics. This itself speaks to the benefit of learning ensembling techniques. The objective of this book is to help you learn ensembles and apply them effectively in real-world situations.

This book starts by explaining why ensemble learning techniques are needed. The objective of Chapter 1 is to build a basic understanding of various ensembling techniques. Chapters 2, 3, and 4, cover various ensemble techniques and are grouped by how we mix training data, models, and combinations. In these chapters, you learn about some of the most important ensemble learning techniques like random forests, bagging, bootstrap aggregating, stacking, and cross validation methods.

Chapter 5 covers ensemble learning libraries. The libraries help you accelerate your experimentation and implementation. Chapter 6 covers techniques for integrating ensembles into real-world machine learning workflows.

This book presents a condensed, easy-to-understand way to learn and apply ensemble learning concepts in real-world use-cases, which otherwise takes a lot of back and forth learning for a budding data scientist. The code in this book (Python scripts) can be used as an extension to your projects or for reference.

CHAPTER 1

Why Ensemble Techniques Are Needed

According to the Cambridge dictionary, an **ensemble** is defined as a group of **things** or people acting or taken together as a whole. The word **ensemble** was first used in the context of musicians who regularly play together. An ensemble of musicians is the sum of individual compositions by multiple musicians. Similarly, in machine learning, **ensemble learning** is a combination of multiple machine learning techniques performed together.

Ensemble learning is fast becoming a go-to standard for getting an accuracy boost in machine learning models in data science. Ensemble methods do this through combining the output of machine learning models in many interesting ways; just like an ensemble of musicians combine their individual performances in multiple different ways to achieve a great composition.

Your role as a data scientist is to become a concertmaster or architect who can leverage the strength of individual machine learning (ML) models and combine them in interesting ways to achieve the ML equivalent of a great composition (i.e., a world-class machine learning model).

© Alok Kumar and Mayank Jain 2020
A. Kumar and M. Jain, *Ensemble Learning for AI Developers*,
https://doi.org/10.1007/978-1-4842-5940-5_1

Let's look at another analogy to build a better understanding of the benefit of ensemble methods. Let's suppose that you want to invest in the stock market. You are interested in a particular stock, but you are not sure about its future outlook, and so you decide to seek advice. You reach out to a financial advisor who has a 75% accuracy in making the right predictions. You decide to check with other financial advisors, who give you similar advice. In a case where each of the advisors suggest that you to buy the stock, what is the accuracy rate of this collective advice?

More often than not, the collective advice of multiple experts beats the accuracy of any one advisor, especially in varied financial situations. Similarly, in machine learning, ensemble methods from multiple machine learning models tend to have a better generalized performance than any single machine learning model, especially in varied conditions/cases or in the long run.

In this book, we take you through ways to combine the output of multiple machine learning models under the umbrella of ensemble learning.

Ensemble learning techniques can be further divided under a broad umbrella of three classes: **mixing training data**, **mixing combinations,** and **mixing models**. We will briefly try to build your understanding of each class.

Mixing Training Data

Anyone who has read about the evolution of species knows that it is very important for any species to have sufficient genetic diversity. Species that have less genetic diversity tend to die out, even if they are fit for the current environment.

One of the reasons for this phenomenon is that even though a species (or current training data) has become expert in its environment, whenever there is an adverse environmental condition, like a new lethal disease, it is not able to adapt, and the species becomes prone to extinction.

One of the ways for any species to develop sufficient genetic diversity is to divide its population and let them evolve inside different environmental conditions. The reason for success in this approach is that dividing the population into different groups and exposing them to different environments leads them to evolve based on the new environments, which leads to increased genetic diversity. This prevents the population from becoming homogeneous, and in adversity, it ensures that at least some of the subgroups of species will survive.

Taking this insight to machine learning leads us to the first ensemble learning variant, which is **Mixing training data** Instead of training a single, large classifier on all the training data, we divide the training data into multiple chunks, and train separate classifiers on each subset of training data. In the end, the output of all of these classifiers are combined (see Figure 1-1).

This approach ensures that classifiers capture sufficient diversity as they are trained (evolve) on a subset of the population. By combining the output of these diverse learners, we are able to achieve superior accuracy compared to a case in which we trained a single learner on a whole population (training data).

This kind of division of training data is called **bagging**. You learn more about this technique in Chapter 2.

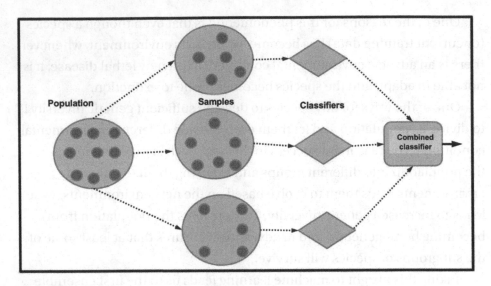

Figure 1-1. *Mixing training data using bagging*

Mixing Combinations

To better understand what mixing, or varying, combinations mean in the context of ensemble learning, let's look at an analogy of the learning process of students in a class.

Suppose that you want a class of students to perform well in all subjects, but we find that some students performed poorly in unit tests. We can identify these students and provide more emphasis to the poorly scored topics so that they come up to par with other students. In order to give more emphasis, we tweak the learning process by adding courses and allocating additional time in the students' weak areas. This ensures that students will perform better in all subjects.

Let's use the same analogy in machine learning. We start out with a collection of learners, in which each ML learner is trained on a particular subset of training objects. If the model learner has a weak performance, we could give more emphasis to that particular learner with increased emphasis where previous learner had weak performance. This combination of learners is known as **boosting**.

Let's look at another different method of mixing machine learning models called **Stacking**. To understand this better imagine stacks of plates on top of each other, each plate on top of stack is built on foundation of plates on bottom of stack. Similarly, in stacking learners, we place one machine learning model on top of the output of another to do stacks of machine learning models. In other words, in this ensemble technique, we train multiple models together to get a predictions/output learner. When we combine these predictions, there could be errors.

In stacking, we treat the result of individual predictions as the next training data. (The first layers of machine learning models/learners are called **base learners**.) We stack another layer of machine learning models/learners on top of the base layers; the second layer is called a **meta learner** (see Figure 1-2). You can think of this technique as stacking one layer of ML learners on top of another ML learner.

Both of these approaches—**boosting** and **stacking**—involve mixing machine learning models in various combinations, which are covered in more detail in Chapter 4.

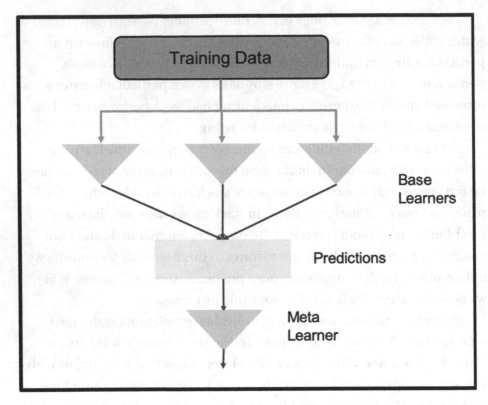

Figure 1-2. Stacking

Mixing Models

The third type of ensemble learning methods involve **varying models**.

Let's consider a scenario in which two kids—Ram and Shyam—are learning science. Ram is receiving all of his learning from a single person, who is a good teacher but teaches in a single, monotonous way. Shyam is taught by multiple teachers, as well as his parents; each teacher boosts his science education by varying their teaching techniques. Does Ram or Shyam have a better probability of getting good grades?

All other things being equal, Shyam has a better chance of being good in science.

It is often observed in children's education that if a child is not dependent on a single person or single way of teaching, he or she will be better off in life. This happens because learning from different people covers the blind spots that are often overlooked by a single person or a single way of teaching.

Again, using this analogy in machine learning, we can train our network in lots of different ways. We can use different models (see Figure 1-3), and even in the case of a single machine learning model, we can use settings/hyperparameters that differ between training runs. Instead of relying on only a single model or single hyperparameter settings for our machine learning tasks, we can combine them together by either training multiple models or by using multiple training runs with different hyperparameter settings. This leads us to have better accuracy and lower bias when compared to using a single model or single settings. The types of ensembling techniques that combine varying models are discussed in Chapter 3.

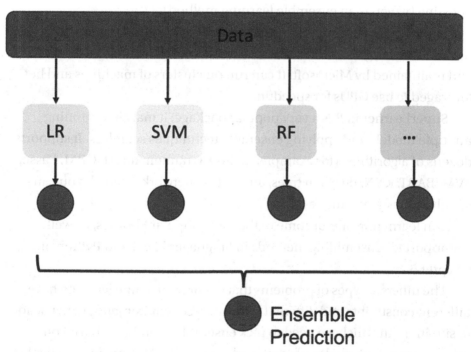

Figure 1-3. *Mixing models*

All the ensemble techniques discussed so far learn are covered in detail in Chapters 2, 3, and 4. They are not helpful until you can apply them in real-world data science problems. One of the major hindrances in adopting many promising concepts is the access to tools and library support. Fortunately, as machine learning researchers have realized the power of ensemble techniques, library support has caught up. Nowadays, many popular ensemble techniques have implementations in Python and R. In addition to ensemble support in general-purpose machine learning libraries like scikit-learn, libraries dedicated to specific ensemble techniques have been developed. Some of these libraries are now standard if you want to achieve state-of-the-art results in data science competitions.

XGBoost is a gradient boosting framework that is used in multiple languages, including C/C++, Python, Java, and R. It can run on multiple operating systems, as well. It can run on a single machine or parallelly run to leverage multiple machines. And it provides fast implementation for boosting (which is an ensemble learning method).

LightGBM is another very popular gradient boosting framework (as of this writing, it has more than 10,000 stars on GitHub) developed and maintained by Microsoft. It can run on clusters of machines and be leveraged to use GPUs for speedup.

SuperLearner in R is a very popular package; it makes combining multiple models and applying ensemble techniques seamless. It supports dozens of algorithms (for example, XGBoost, random forest, GBM, Lasso, SVM, BART, KNN, decision trees, and neural networks), which you can simultaneously run and test.

You learn more about some of the most popular libraries, as well as support for ensembling methods in languages like R and Python, in Chapter 5.

The different types of problems that occur in machine learning have different constraints and different performance requirements, which lead to situations in which we need to pick ensemble techniques based on requirements. Knowledge of what works and what does not in a particular problem domain is very helpful to a practitioner. In Chapter 6 (tips and best practices), we apply different ensemble techniques in different problem domains (e.g., image classification, natural language processing, etc.).

One of the reasons for huge recent popularity of ensemble learning techniques is the boost it gives to your problem, if you are a team working on a challenging machine learning problem with the goal of beating state of the art, with ensemble methods you each work on your individual approach and then can combine results by simple ensembling methods. This is also the pattern followed by most recent winners in various competitive machine learning contests.

Take the example of a safe driver prediction competition held on Kaggle in 2017, in which more than 5000 teams competed for correctly predicting whether a driver would file an insurance claim next year based on various parameters. The winning solution was developed by Michael Jahrer; it was a blend of six different machine learning models. One model used gradient boosting from the LightGBM library; he then combined the result with five neural networks with different parameters. By using this ensemble of results, Jahrer was able to achieve the top ranking—and the $25,000 prize money.

Most of the winners of almost all recent data science competitions relied on ensembling techniques to achieve their results.

Another example is the Avito Demand Prediction Challenge that was held in September 2019. The goal was to predict the demand for classified ads based on different ad parameters, such as an included image, the text description, and so forth. More than 1800 teams took part in the competition for a $25,000 prize. The winning team named their entry "Dance with Ensembles" and credited ensemble methods for their success in the competition. The team of four worked independently, with each team member using many ensemble-based methods, including LightGBM combined with traditional neural networks methods with different parameters. Each of the team members later combined their results by using the power of ensembling.

You can browse blog posts on the winning stories on many competitive coding platforms, like Kaggle. Almost all of them boosted their results or combined different algorithms using ensemble techniques. This is a strong indicator of the success of ensemble learning in real-world machine learning problems.

Summary

The following is a quick recap of what we covered in this chapter.

- A basic answer to **What is ensemble learning, and why is it used?**

- A brief introduction to ensemble learning using **mixing of training data**.

- A brief introduction to ensemble methods where we **mix models.**

- A brief introduction to ensemble learning, where we **mix combinations** of models with examples of boosting and stacking.

- A brief introduction to some machine learning libraries.

- The ways that people are using advanced ensemble learning techniques to achieve state- of-the-art results in real-world problems and competitive data science competitions.

In the next chapter, you learn how to start to build ensemble-based methods, starting with methods that mix training data for ensembling.

CHAPTER 2

Mixing Training Data

In Chapter 1, you learned how the role of a data scientist is similar to a concertmaster who uses his ensemble of orchestra and instruments to compose a beautiful composition. Similarly, a data scientist has multiple ensemble tools at his disposal if he wants to squeeze a world-class performance out of his data and models. In this chapter, the main goal is to learn different ways to mix training data to get ensemble models.

The following are the goals for this chapter.

- Build an intuitive understanding of how mixing training data can lead to good performance in ensemble learning

- Introduce decision trees

- Look at an example implementation of a decision tree using scikit-learn

- Introduce random forests as a collection of decision trees

- Learn about sampling datasets and two variants: sampling without replacement and sampling with replacement by using code examples

- Learn about bagging (bootstrap aggregating) by using code examples

- Learn about cross-validation techniques: k-fold cross-validation and stratified k-fold cross-validation

© Alok Kumar and Mayank Jain 2020
A. Kumar and M. Jain, *Ensemble Learning for AI Developers*,
https://doi.org/10.1007/978-1-4842-5940-5_2

Let's start by learning why mixing data is useful. Charles Darwin discovered that a species is more vulnerable to extinction if it does not have sufficient genetic diversity. Why is that so? A species is more vulnerable to unexpected natural disasters and diseases if all members have the same genetics because everyone is equally vulnerable to unexpected events.

How can a species develop sufficient genetic diversity naturally? One of the natural ways to develop sufficient genetic diversity happens when the population is divided and must evolve inside different environmental conditions. This ensures that if a species encounters an adverse and unexpected environment, at least a subset of the species has more resilience; so overall, the survival of the species is ensured. Dividing a population into different groups and exposing them to different environments leads the population to evolve slightly differently, which leads to increased genetic diversity.

Using the same knowledge and applying it to machine learning, if you train a single model with whole training data, the machine learning model might perform alright if the real-world testing data has a distribution similar to the training data. If you use data that does not sufficiently look like the distribution from the training data, you could face issues. To solve this issue, it is a good idea to divide the training data into different subsets and train the multiple models on different subsets of data. By virtue of having different training data distribution, each of these models has a slightly different inference (real-world performance) characteristics. Then we can combine these models by ensembling them to get better results than a single model. This is called **mixing training data**.

Decision Trees

Let's learn how to mix data by using an example of a machine learning model called a **decision tree** (see Figure 2-1).

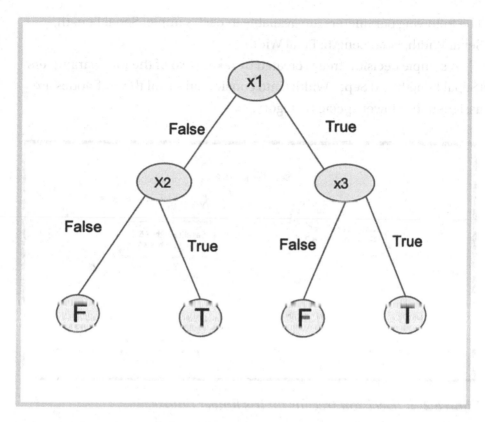

Figure 2-1. *Simple decision tree*

A decision tree is a top-down flowchart-like method, in which you start from the top node. Each node represents a decision that needs to be taken based on one or more parameters/variables. You traverse these nodes until you reach sufficient depth, which is based on the number of parameters that you want to train on.

Let's start with an example dataset to discover how you can apply a decision tree to it.

The iris flower dataset is a widely used standard dataset inside the machine learning community. Figure 2-2 shows the decision tree for the iris flower dataset. Our task is to classify iris flowers into three different flower species This dataset has 50 samples for each of the three iris species.

The following parameters are available in each sample: Sepal Length, Sepal Width, Petal Length, Petal Width.

A sample decision tree is created by taking two of the four parameters (Sepal Length and Sepal Width) into consideration; all the leaf nodes are assigned to a flower species category.

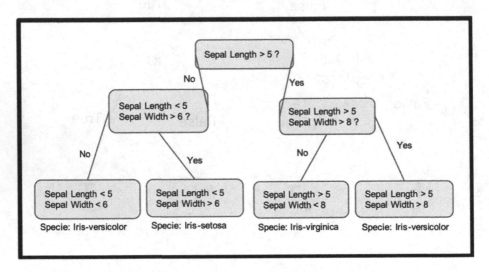

Figure 2-2. *Decision tree for an iris flower dataset*

A decision tree is applied in practice by taking a sample from a dataset. Tree traversal starts from the top node partition sample and goes into buckets based on conditions at each node. Each node is based on an answer and then takes a left or a right node. It proceeds from there by continuously applying condition testing. You eventually reach the bottom leaf nodes, where you get a final assignment.

To train a decision tree, you can use the scikit-learn Python library. Listing 2-1 shows how to train a decision tree by using the scikit-learn library in Python.

Listing 2-1. Training a Decision Tree Using scikit-learn

```
from sklearn.datasets import load_iris
from sklearn.tree import DecisionTreeClassifier
from sklearn.model_selection import train_test_split

X, y = load_iris(return_X_y=True)
train_X, test_X, train_Y, test_Y = train_test_split(X, y,
test_size = 0.2, random_state = 123)
tree = DecisionTreeClassifier()
tree.fit(train_X, train_Y)
print(tree.score(test_X, test_Y))
# Output: 0.9333333333333333
```

The greater the depth of a decision tree, the greater the accuracy of the training dataset.

But there are major problems with using decision trees. To get sufficient accuracy of your dataset, you need to have a tree with bigger (more depth) trees, but as you increase the depth of the tree, you start to encounter overfitting, which leads to lower accuracy in your test dataset. So you have to be content with either a less accurate, shallower decision tree or an overfitted tree with more depth.

One of the reasons for this issue is that the variables used using in making decisions may not be sufficiently discriminatory for a global perspective.

One way to solve this problem is to have multiple decision trees instead of one. Each decision tree should have a different set of variables or a subset of training data. Then, the output of the decision trees is combined in a random forest (see Figure 2-3).

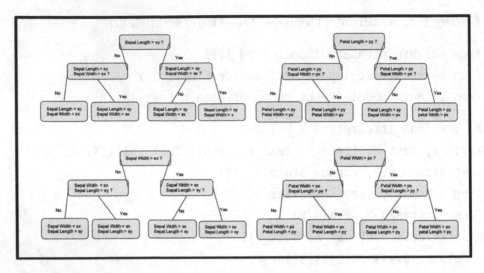

Figure 2-3. *Random forest with number of decision trees = 4 for iris flower dataset*

As the name suggests, a **random forest** consists of collection of decision trees, with each tree trained on a different set of training data.

Listing 2-2 is the code snippet for a random forest in Python scikit-learn.

Listing 2-2. Training Random Forest Using scikit-learn with Number of Decision Trees = 4

```
from sklearn.datasets import load_iris
from sklearn.ensemble import RandomForestClassifier
from sklearn.model_selection import train_test_split

X, y = load_iris(return_X_y=True)
train_X, test_X, train_Y, test_Y = train_test_split(X, y,
test_size = 0.1, random_state = 123)
forest = RandomForestClassifier(n_estimators=8)
forest = forest.fit(train_X, train_Y)
print(forest.score(test_X, test_Y))
```

```
# Output: 1.0
rf_output = forest.predict(test_X)
print(rf_output)
# Output: [1 2 2 1 0 2 1 0 0 1 2 0 1 2 2]
```

A random forest from a set of decision trees offers the best of both worlds: better accuracy with shallower decision trees and less chance of overfitting.

A random forest is one example of ensembles of decision trees. We take a single machine learning model (a decision tree) and train it with a mix of different training data and parameters to make an ensemble model.

How do we combine training data in different ways to make a combined ensemble method? The devil is in the details!

Let's start with learning some basics, which you can skip or skim if you already know about it.

First, we talk about sampling, which can be categorized in two ways: sampling without replacement (WOR) and sampling with replacement.

Sampling a Dataset

Sampling is the act of dividing a dataset. Let's use an analogy of a fisherman who is fishing in a small pond with a limited number of fish. He wants to group the fish into different divisions. There are two ways he can do this: *sampling without replacement* and *sampling with replacement.*

Sampling Without Replacement (WOR)

Let's say that the fisherman has two buckets. He takes the fish he caught from the pond and throws them into either of the two buckets. His dataset is divided into two distinct buckets. Using this method, there is never a case in which a single fish belongs in both buckets.

The method of sampling where you divide your dataset into two or more disjointed sets is called **sampling without replacement** (see Figure 2-4).

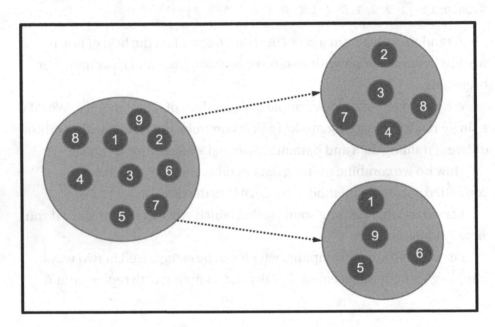

Figure 2-4. *Sampling without replacement (WOR). There are no common samples from the original dataset*

Listing 2-3 shows how to get samples without replacement in Python's scikit-learn.

Listing 2-3. Sampling Without Replacement in scikit-learn

```
from sklearn.utils import resample
import numpy as np

# Random seed fixed so result could be replicated by Reader
np.random.seed(123)
#data to be sampled
data = [1, 2, 3, 4, 5, 6, 7, 8, 9]
```

```
# Number of divisions needed
num_divisions = 2
list_of_data_divisions = []
for x in range(0, num_divisions):
    sample = resample(data, replace=False, n_samples=5)
    list_of_data_divisions.append(sample)
print('Samples', list_of_data_divisions)
# Output: Samples [[8, 1, 6, 7, 4], [4, 6, 5, 3, 8]]
```

Sampling with Replacement (WR)

Let's use the fisherman analogy again. This time, the fisherman has two
diaries. As he catches each fish, he marks it with a number and enters this
number in either of the diaries. But there is a twist: after he catches the
fish and numbers it in a diary, he throws the fish back into the pond. He
continues to catch fish. If a fish already has a number assigned, he enters
the same number in either of the diaries. He repeats this process until all
the fish in the pond have a number assigned. In this process, there might
be cases where a single fish entry could be in both diaries. This process
of sampling, in which you divide a dataset into two sets but the sets do
not need to be disjointed is called **sampling with replacement**. You can
take a look at Listing 2-4 for sample code for Sampling with replacement
implemented using scikit learn.

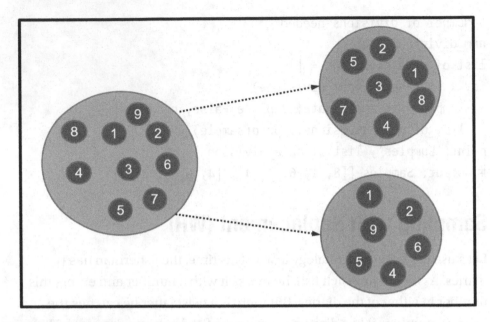

Figure 2-5. *Sampling with replacement (WR). Note some of the samples from the original dataset are common in both samples (item 1,4,5)*

Listing 2-4. Sampling with Replacement in scikit-learn

```
from sklearn.utils import resample
import numpy as np

# Random seed fixed so result could be replicated by Reader
np.random.seed(123)
# data to be sampled
data = [1, 2, 3, 4, 5, 6, 7, 8, 9]
# Number of divisions needed
num_divisions = 3
list_of_data_divisions = []
```

```
for x in range(0, num_divisions):
    sample = resample(data, replace=True, n_samples=4)
    list_of_data_divisions.append(sample)

print("Samples", list_of_data_divisions)
# Output: Samples [[3, 3, 7, 2], [4, 7, 2, 1], [2, 1, 1, 4]]
```

Bagging (Bootstrap Aggregating)

You are now familiar with sampling a dataset with or without replacement. This section introduces one of the most important ensemble techniques: **bagging**. Bagging is a short form of bootstrap aggregating. It is an ensemble technique that divides a dataset into n samples with replacement. Each of the divided n samples are then trained separately into n separate machine learning models. Then the output of all the separate models are combined into one single output by using voting (see Figure 2-6).

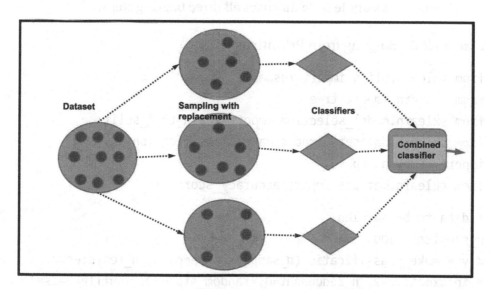

Figure 2-6. *Bagging with sampling with replacement*

As you can see, the bagging technique ensures that each classifier gets random samples, which ensures a diverse set of trained models. These diverse models provide a much better performing model than any of the individual models.

Bagging consists of three steps: bootstrapping, training, and aggregating. First, the bootstrapping step divides a dataset into n samples, with each sample a subset of the total training data. Each of these samples has its sampling done by using sampling by replacement techniques. As we discussed earlier, sampling with replacement ensures that the sampling is truly random; the composition of one sample does not depend on another sample.

Next is the training step, in which you train individual models on these samples separately. This step ensures that you get lots of relatively weak machine learning models trained on each sample.

The third step is aggregating, in which you combine the results of all the weak classifiers using methods like voting (which you learn in Chapter 3).

Listing 2-5 is sample code that uses all three bagging steps.

Listing 2-5. Bagging from Primitives

```
from sklearn.utils import resample
from sklearn import tree
from sklearn.model_selection import train_test_split
from sklearn.datasets import make_classification
import numpy as np
from sklearn.metrics import accuracy_score

# data to be sampled
n_samples = 100
X,y = make_classification(n_samples=n_samples, n_features=4,
n_informative=2, n_redundant=0, random_state=0, shuffle=False)
```

```
#divide data into train and test set
X_train, X_test, y_train, y_test =  train_test_split(X, y,
test_size = 0.1, random_state = 123)

# Number of divisions needed
num_divisions = 3
list_of_data_divisions = []
# Divide data into divisions
for x in range(0, num_divisions):
   X_train_sample, y_train_sample = resample(X_train, y_train,
replace=True, n_samples=7)
   sample = [X_train_sample, y_train_sample]
   list_of_data_divisions.append(sample)

#print(list_of_data_divisions)
# Learn a Classifier for each data divisions
learners = []
for data_division in list_of_data_divisions:
   data_x = data_division[0]
   data_y = data_division[1]
   decision_tree = tree.DecisionTreeClassifier()
   decision_tree.fit(data_x, data_y)
   learners.append(decision_tree)

# Combine output of all classifiers using voting
predictions = []
for i in range(len(y_test)):
   counts = [0 for _ in range(num_divisions)]
   for j , learner in enumerate(learners):
       prediction = learner.predict([X_test[i]])
```

```
    if prediction == 1:
        counts[j] = counts[j] + 1
  final_predictions = np.argmax(counts)
  predictions.append(final_predictions)
```

```
accuracy = accuracy_score(y_test, predictions)
print("Accuracy:", accuracy)
# Output: Accuracy: 0.9
```

You can directly call the Bagging classifier from the scikit-learn library. Listing 2-6 is sample code from a scikit-learn implementation of the Bagging classifier.

Listing 2-6. Bagging scikit-learn

```
from sklearn.svm import SVC
from sklearn.ensemble import BaggingClassifier
from sklearn.model_selection import train_test_split
from sklearn.datasets import make_classification

X, y = make_classification(n_samples=100, n_features=4,
                           n_informative=2, n_redundant=0,
                           random_state=0, shuffle=False)

#divide data into train and test set
X_train, X_test, y_train, y_test =  train_test_split(X, y,
test_size = 0.2, random_state = 123)
clf = BaggingClassifier(base_estimator=SVC(),
n_estimators=10, random_state=0).fit(X_train, y_train)
print(clf.score(X_test, y_test))
# Output: 0.9
```

k-Fold Cross-Validation

Moving further into our exploration of resampling-based machine learning techniques, one of the most popular techniques is cross-validation, especially K Fold cross-validation. Machine learning researchers often encounter a situation where they achieve good accuracy in a training dataset, even in the test dataset; but in the application of the same model in a real-world situation or on another hidden test dataset, they lose out due to suboptimal accuracy.

This is especially problematic for people who do competitive machine learning on sites like Kaggle. One of the primary reasons for this is because the provided validation set does not have all the different distributions that are possible in a real-world situation. A very effective solution is to apply a sampling technique in the division of training and the validation dataset itself. This approach is called cross validation.

One of the most popular cross-validation techniques is *k*-fold cross-validation (see Figure 2-7). In this approach, you divide validation and the training dataset by using sampling without replacement, iteratively. *k* represents the number of divisions applied to the dataset. For example, with $k = 10$, we divide the dataset into 10 different parts; 9/10 of the dataset is applied to training and 1/10 is applied to testing the accuracy of the dataset. But the division does not stop there. The process is repeated 10 times, in which each test and training division is changed and the overall accuracy is recalculated. The final accuracy of your model is calculated by averaging each of the individual accuracy figures.

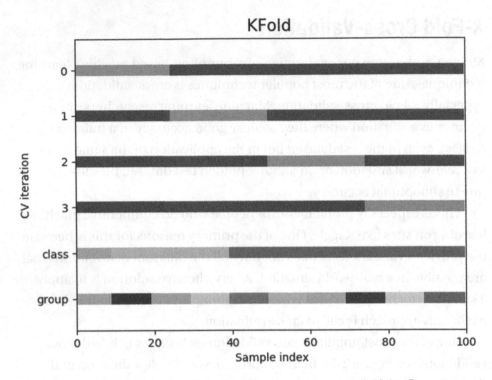

Figure 2-7. *k-fold cross-validation (Source: https://scikit-learn.org/ stable/auto_examples/model_selection/plot_cv_indices.html#sphx- glr-auto-examples-model-selection-plot-cv-indices-py)*

Listing 2-7 is sample code for applying this technique using scikit-learn.

Listing 2-7. k-Fold Cross-Validation

```
import numpy as np
from sklearn.model_selection import KFold

X = np.array([[1, 2], [3, 4], [1, 2], [3, 4]])
y = np.array([1, 2, 3, 4])
kf = KFold(n_splits=2)
kf.get_n_splits(X)
print(kf)
```

```
# Output:
# KFold(n_splits=2, random_state=None, shuffle=False)
for train_index, test_index in kf.split(X):
    print("TRAIN:", train_index, "TEST:", test_index)
    X_train, X_test = X[train_index], X[test_index]
    y_train, y_test = y[train_index], y[test_index]

# Output:
# TRAIN: [2 3] TEST: [0 1]
# TRAIN: [0 1] TEST: [2 3]
```

Stratified *k*-Fold Cross-Validation

Stratified *k*-fold cross-validation is another subvariant of *k*-fold cross
validation. Like *k*-fold validation, you divide a dataset into different sample
sets, and rotate testing and training the sets *k* times for uniform cross-
validation. But there is a twist with the initial sampling. In the stratified
k-fold cross-validation technique, you make sure that each of the initial *k*
samples have a data distribution such that each of the divided samples has
a distribution similar to the overall dataset.

Figure 2-8 shows 100 randomly generated input data points. Three
classes are split unevenly across the data points, and 10 "groups" are split
evenly across the data points. In other words, let's say in your overall
dataset there are three classes: class A, class B, and class C. Each of these
classes has samples in proportions of 30%, 50%, and 20%, respectively.
In a stratified *k*-fold cross-validation technique, you have to ensure that
if you divide this dataset in *k* = 5 folds, then each of the five folds have
similar 30%, 50%, and 20% of samples from class A, class B, and class C,
respectively.

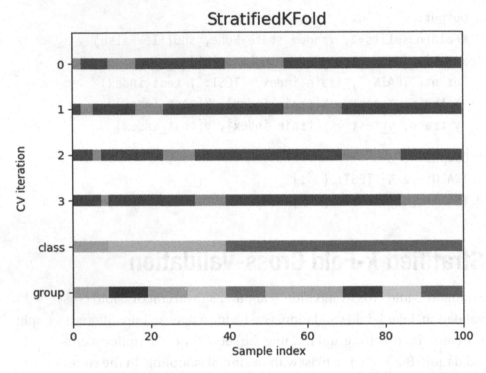

Figure 2-8. *Stratified k-fold cross-validation (Source: https://scikit-learn.org/stable/auto_examples/model_selection/plot_cv_indices.html#sphx-glr-auto-examples-model-selection-plot-cv-indices-py)*

Listing 2-8 is Python sample code on how to apply a stratified *k*-fold cross-validation technique using scikit-learn.

Listing 2-8. Stratified k-Fold Cross-Validation

```python
import numpy as np
from sklearn.model_selection import StratifiedKFold

X = np.array([[1, 2], [3, 4], [1, 2], [3, 4]])
y = np.array([0, 0, 1, 1])

skf = StratifiedKFold(n_splits=2)
skf.get_n_splits(X, y)
```

```
print(skf)
# Output:
# StratifiedKFold(n_splits=2, random_state=None, shuffle=False)

for train_index, test_index in skf.split(X, y):
    print("TRAIN:", train_index, "TEST:", test_index)
    X_train, X_test = X[train_index], X[test_index]
    y_train, y_test = y[train_index], y[test_index]

# Output:
# TRAIN: [1 3] TEST: [0 2]
# TRAIN: [0 2] TEST: [1 3]
```

Summary

Let's do a quick recap of what you learned in this chapter.

- Combing mixed data to make performance ensemble models

- Decision trees and random forests by using code examples

- Sampling data

- Two primary variants of sampling: sampling without replacement and sampling with replacement

- Bagging, or the bootstrap aggregating technique, using sampling with replacement

- Cross-validation techniques namely k-fold cross-validation as well as stratified k-fold cross-validation

- Applying these techniques through problems with code examples in scikit-learn

CHAPTER 3

Mixing Models

In Chapter 2, you learned how to divide and mix training data in different ways to build ensemble models, which perform better than a model that was trained on an undivided dataset.

In this chapter, you learn different ways to assemble. Unlike the mixing training data approach, the **mixing models** approach uses the same dataset in different machine learning models and then combines the results in different ways to get better performing models.

First, let's look at this chapter's goals.

- Introduce and explain mixing models based on ensemble

- Introduce voting ensembles

- Introduce and explain soft and hard voting ensembles with code examples

- Learn about hyperparameter tuning ensembles

- Examine a sample implementation of hyperparameter tuning with random forest

- Learn about horizontal voting ensembles

- Examine a sample implementation of horizontal voting ensemble on CIFAR dataset using scikit-learn and Keras

- Introduce the snapshot ensemble technique used with cyclic learning rates

© Alok Kumar and Mayank Jain 2020
A. Kumar and M. Jain, *Ensemble Learning for AI Developers*,
https://doi.org/10.1007/978-1-4842-5940-5_3

Instead of relying on a single model, in this chapter, you train a dataset
of various machine learning models together (see Figure 3-1), and then
combine the results from these models by using different techniques.
First, you learn ways to combine the output of differently trained models
in the form of voting and averaging. Next, you look at **hyperparameter
tuning ensembles**, in which you learn how to use the same model trained
with different hyperparameter settings, and then combine the results to
get a better model. Lastly, you will learn about the relatively lesser known
techniques of **horizontal voting ensemble** and **snapshot ensembles**,
which are gaining a foothold in the machine learning community for their
potential.

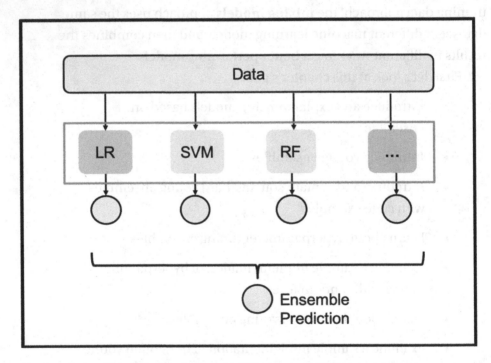

Figure 3-1. *Combining/mixing different models*

Voting Ensembles

Hard Voting

Let's first look at one of the most popular ensemble learning techniques: voting ensembles. Voting ensembles train different machine learning models. Take a look at Figure 3-1 again, in which the same data is trained on three different machine learning models— logistic regression, support vector machine (SVM), and random forest. The output of these three models is combined to get an ensemble prediction. The first question from any practitioner is how to actually combine the results of these models. One of the simplest answers is to take inspiration from one of the oldest tried and tested techniques: voting. Just as voting is done to elect our leaders, where the majority vote of a diverse set of people selects the official, we conduct an election using different machine learning models. If it is a classification problem, each ML model votes for a particular category. In majority voting, the class that earns the most votes is the preferred class. It is widely observed that the resulting class often has higher accuracy than any single model.

The dataset in Listing 3-1 is trained using three machine learning models: k-nearest neighbors (KNN), random forest, and logistic regression using the scikit-learn Python library. Their output is then combined using a Voting classifier implemented in the scikit-learn library. If you measure the resultant accuracy of each of the individual models, as well as the combined model on the test dataset, you get a very good boost in accuracy. We encourage you to run the code as an exercise and check the accuracy of the individual models and the combined models.

A major helper function that you can use for this is the Voting classifier class from the sklearn.ensemble package of the scikit-learn library.

Listing 3-1. Max Voting Ensemble

```python
from sklearn.model_selection import train_test_split
from sklearn.model_selection import GridSearchCV
from sklearn.datasets import load_breast_cancer
import numpy as np

X, y = load_breast_cancer(return_X_y=True)
X_train, X_test, y_train, y_test = train_test_split(X, y,
test_size=0.3, stratify=y, random_state=123)
### k-Nearest Neighbors (k-NN)
from sklearn.neighbors import KNeighborsClassifier

knn = KNeighborsClassifier()
params_knn = {'n_neighbors': np.arange(1, 25)}
knn_gs = GridSearchCV(knn, params_knn, cv=5)
knn_gs.fit(X_train, y_train)
knn_best = knn_gs.best_estimator_

### Random Forest Classifier
from sklearn.ensemble import RandomForestClassifier

rf = RandomForestClassifier(random_state=0)
params_rf = {'n_estimators': [50, 100, 200]}
rf_gs = GridSearchCV(rf, params_rf, cv=5)
rf_gs.fit(X_train, y_train)
rf_best = rf_gs.best_estimator_

### Logistic Regression
from sklearn.linear_model import LogisticRegression

log_reg = LogisticRegression(random_state=123,
solver='liblinear', penalty='l2', max_iter=5000)
C = np.logspace(1, 4, 10)
params_lr = dict(C=C)
```

```
lr_gs = GridSearchCV(log_reg, params_lr, cv=5, verbose=0)
lr_gs.fit(X_train, y_train)
lr_best = lr_gs.best_estimator_

# combine all three Voting Ensembles
from sklearn.ensemble import VotingClassifier

estimators=[('knn', knn_best), ('rf', rf_best), ('log_reg',
lr_best)]
ensemble = VotingClassifier(estimators, voting='soft')
ensemble.fit(X_train, y_train)
print("knn_gs.score: ", knn_best.score(X_test, y_test))
# Output: knn_gs.score:   0.9239766081871345
print("rf_gs.score: ", rf_best.score(X_test, y_test))
# Output: rf_gs.score:   0.9766081871345029
print("log_reg.score: ", lr_best.score(X_test, y_test))
# Output: log_reg.score:   0.9590643274853801
print("ensemble.score: ", ensemble.score(X_test, y_test))
# Output: ensemble.score:   0.9649122807017544
```

Averaging/Soft Voting

Averaging is another way to combine the output of different classifiers.
The major difference between voting and averaging is that in averaging,
we take the prediction probability of each class separately from the model
and then combine the resulting probabilities by taking the average of these
predictions. This combination method is called **soft voting**.

In Listing 3-2, the initial steps to train different models are the same,
but instead of using the Voting classifier, we do inference of our model
on our test dataset, take out the prediction probabilities of each class,
and then take out the average of all the probabilities as a resultant class
probability on the test dataset.

Note that we have assigned equal weight to all the models when calculating the average output. If we think a particular model is more important than the other models, however, we can increase the weight of that particular model and decrease the weight of all the other models. This approach is called **weighted averaging**.

Listing 3-2. Averaging

```
from sklearn.model_selection import train_test_split
from sklearn.model_selection import GridSearchCV
from sklearn.datasets import load_breast_cancer
import numpy as np

X, y = load_breast_cancer(return_X_y=True)
X_train, X_test, y_train, y_test = train_test_split(X, y,
test_size=0.3, stratify=y, random_state=0)
### k-Nearest Neighbors (k-NN)
from sklearn.neighbors import KNeighborsClassifier

knn = KNeighborsClassifier()
params_knn = {'n_neighbors': np.arange(1, 25)}
knn_gs = GridSearchCV(knn, params_knn, cv=5)
knn_gs.fit(X_train, y_train)
knn_best = knn_gs.best_estimator_
knn_gs_predictions = knn_gs.predict(X_test)

### Random Forest Classifier
from sklearn.ensemble import RandomForestClassifier

rf = RandomForestClassifier(random_state=0)
params_rf = {'n_estimators': [50, 100, 200]}
rf_gs = GridSearchCV(rf, params_rf, cv=5)
rf_gs.fit(X_train, y_train)
rf_best = rf_gs.best_estimator_
rf_gs_predictions = rf_gs.predict(X_test)
```

```
### Logistic Regression
from sklearn.linear_model import LogisticRegression

log_reg = LogisticRegression(random_state=123,
solver='liblinear', penalty='l2', max_iter=5000)
C = np.logspace(1, 4, 10)
params_lr = dict(C=C)
lr_gs = GridSearchCV(log_reg, params_lr, cv=5, verbose=0)
lr_gs.fit(X_train, y_train)
lr_best = lr_gs.best_estimator_
log_reg_predictions = lr_gs.predict(X_test)

# combine all three by averaging the Ensembles results
average_prediction = (log_reg_predictions + knn_gs_predictions
+ rf_gs_predictions)/3.0

# Alternatively combine all through using VotingClassifier with
voting='soft' parameter
# combine all three Voting Ensembles
from sklearn.ensemble import VotingClassifier

estimators=[('knn', knn_best), ('rf', rf_best), ('log_reg', lr_best)]
ensemble = VotingClassifier(estimators, voting='soft')
ensemble.fit(X_train, y_train)
print("knn_gs.score: ", knn_gs.score(X_test, y_test))
# Output: knn_gs.score:  0.9239766081871345
print("rf_gs.score: ", rf_gs.score(X_test, y_test))
# Output: rf_gs.score:  0.9532163742690059
print("log_reg.score: ", lr_gs.score(X_test, y_test))
# Output: log_reg.score:  0.9415204678362573
print("ensemble.score: ", ensemble.score(X_test, y_test))
# Output: ensemble.score:  0.9473684210526315
```

Apart from calculating predicted probability manually, if you want straightforward results using averaging you can again use the VotingClassifier class from sklearn.ensemble package. But instead of passing on the `voting='hard'` parameter, use the `voting='soft'` parameter.

Hyperparameter Tuning Ensembles

So far, you have seen two examples of training different machine learning models and combining their output. Hyperparameter tuning ensemble is another way to get ensemble output. Instead of relying on different models to make ensemble models, you use a good machine learning model and train this model using different hyperparameter settings.

Figure 3-2 uses the same machine learning model—a random forest, but instantiates three instances of this model with different hyperparameter settings. In the random forest algorithm, one of the most important hyperparameters is the number of trees, called *n_estimators* in the scikit-learn API. Three different random forests are trained with varying numbers of trees (10, 50, and 100, respectively). Similarly, the number of training data cycles, or **epochs**, that this model is trained on also differs for each of the three instances. The output of these instances is then combined using previous techniques (e.g., voting or averaging) to get an ensembled output.

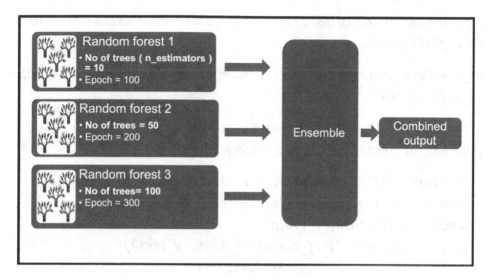

Figure 3-2. *Hyperparameter tuning ensembles*

Listing 3 3 trains a random forest using three different parameters (i.e., the number of trees or m_estimators) to get a combined result using voting.

Listing 3-3. Hyperparameter Tuning Ensembles

```
from sklearn.model_selection import train_test_split
from sklearn.model_selection import GridSearchCV
from sklearn.datasets import load_breast_cancer
import numpy as np

X, y = load_breast_cancer(return_X_y=True)
X_train, X_test, y_train, y_test = train_test_split(X, y,
test_size=0.3, stratify=y, random_state=0)

### Random Forest Classifier
from sklearn.ensemble import RandomForestClassifier

rf_1 = RandomForestClassifier(random_state=0, n_estimators=10)
rf_1.fit(X_train, y_train)
```

```
rf_2 = RandomForestClassifier(random_state=0, n_estimators=50)
rf_2.fit(X_train, y_train)

rf_3 = RandomForestClassifier(random_state=0, n_estimators=100)
rf_3.fit(X_train, y_train)

# combine all three Voting Ensembles
from sklearn.ensemble import VotingClassifier

estimators = [('rf_1', rf_1), ('rf_2', rf_2), ('rf_3', rf_3)]
ensemble = VotingClassifier(estimators, voting='hard')
ensemble.fit(X_train, y_train)
print("rf_1.score: ", rf_1.score(X_test, y_test))
# Output: rf_1.score: 0.935672514619883
print("rf_2.score: ", rf_2.score(X_test, y_test))
# Output: rf_1.score: 0.9473684210526315
print("rf_3.score: ", rf_3.score(X_test, y_test))
# Output: rf_3.score: 0.9532163742690059
print("ensemble.score: ", ensemble.score(X_test, y_test))
# Output: ensemble.score:  0.9415204678362573
```

Horizontal Voting Ensembles

The previous examples of mixing models—voting, averaging, and hyperparameter tuning—work very effectively in classical machine learning. But sometimes we encounter situations (especially in deep learning) in which our training data size, training data time, and model size are very large. There might be cases where training takes too much computation and time. In these cases, it is not practically possible to train multiple ensembles of models in a short amount of time. For example, a deep learning model could take two or three days in convergence on a powerful GPU machine if trained on a dataset like ImageNet. In situations like this, it is often impractical or cost-prohibitive to train multiple models and multiple instances of the same model with different hyperparameters. So, one of the techniques that you can try is **horizontal voting**.

Whenever you run a long machine learning job, you could encounter dilemma that after certain number of epoch of training if model accuracy has stopped improving or not. In cases like this, it becomes difficult to select an accurate epoch time for a model. In a horizontal voting ensemble (see Figure 3-3), you save models after a minimum number of epochs (here, epoch = 300). The resulting models are recombined using voting techniques to get an accuracy boost.

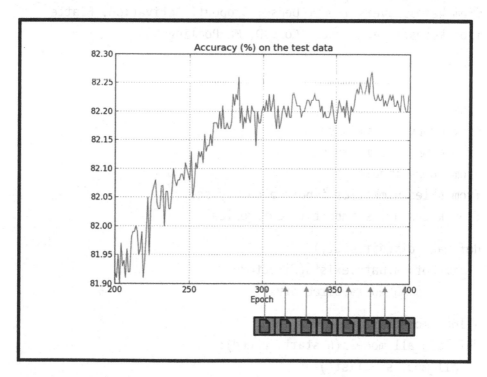

Figure 3-3. *Horizontal voting ensembles*

Take a look at Listing 3-4 where we have implemented horizontal voting ensembles using keras, tensorflow and scikit learn libraries.

Listing 3-4. Horizontal Voting Ensembles

```
#!pip install q keras==2.3.1 tensorflow==1.15.2
import keras
from keras.datasets import cifar10
from keras.preprocessing.image import ImageDataGenerator
from keras.models import Sequential
from keras.models import load_model
from keras.layers import Dense, Dropout, Activation, Flatten
from keras.layers import Conv2D, MaxPooling2D

import os
import numpy
from numpy import array
from numpy import argmax
from numpy import mean
from numpy import std
from sklearn.metrics import accuracy_score
from keras.utils import to_categorical

def make_dir(directory):
    if not os.path.exists(directory):
        os.makedirs(directory)

# load models from file
def load_all_models(n_start, n_end):
    all_models = list()
    for epoch in range(n_start, n_end):
        # define filename for this ensemble
        filename = "models/model_" + str(epoch) + ".h5"
```

```
        # load model from file
        model = load_model(filename)
        # add to list of members
        all_models.append(model)
        print(">loaded %s" % filename)
    return all_models

# make an ensemble prediction for multi-class classification
def ensemble_predictions(members, testX):
    # make predictions
    yhats = [model.predict(testX) for model in members]
    yhats = array(yhats)
    # sum across ensemble members
    summed = numpy.sum(yhats, axis=0)
    # argmax across classes
    result = argmax(summed, axis=1)
    return result

# evaluate a specific number of members in an ensemble
def evaluate_n_members(members, n_members, testX, testy):
    # select a subset of members
    subset = members[:n_members]
    # make prediction
    yhat = ensemble_predictions(subset, testX)
    # calculate accuracy
    return accuracy_score(testy, yhat)

make_dir("models")
batch_size = 32
num_classes = 10
epochs = 100
num_predictions = 20
model_name = "keras_cifar10_trained_model.h5"
```

```
# The data, split between train and test sets:
(x_train, y_train), (x_test, y_test) = cifar10.load_data()
print("x_train shape:", x_train.shape)
print(x_train.shape[0], "train samples")
print(x_test.shape[0], "test samples")

# Convert class vectors to binary class matrices.
y_train = keras.utils.to_categorical(y_train, num_classes)
y_test = keras.utils.to_categorical(y_test, num_classes)

model = Sequential()
model.add(Conv2D(32, (3, 3), padding="same", input_shape=x
_train.shape[1:]))
model.add(Activation("relu"))
model.add(Conv2D(32, (3, 3)))
model.add(Activation("relu"))
model.add(MaxPooling2D(pool_size=(2, 2)))
model.add(Dropout(0.25))

model.add(Conv2D(64, (3, 3), padding="same"))
model.add(Activation("relu"))
model.add(Conv2D(64, (3, 3)))
model.add(Activation("relu"))
model.add(MaxPooling2D(pool_size=(2, 2)))
model.add(Dropout(0.25))

model.add(Flatten())
model.add(Dense(512))
model.add(Activation("relu"))
model.add(Dropout(0.5))
model.add(Dense(num_classes))
model.add(Activation("softmax"))
# initiate RMSprop optimizer
```

```python
opt = keras.optimizers.RMSprop(learning_rate=0.0001,
decay=1e-6)
# Let's train the model using RMSprop
model.compile(loss="categorical_crossentropy", optimizer=opt,
metrics=["accuracy"])
x_train = x_train.astype("float32")
x_test = x_test.astype("float32")
x_train /= 255
x_test /= 255
# fit model
n_epochs, n_save_after = 15, 10
for i in range(n_epochs):
    # fit model for a single epoch
    print("Epoch: ", i)
    model.fit(
        x_train,
        y_train,
        batch_size=batch_size,
        epochs=1,
        validation_data=(x_test, y_test),
        shuffle=True,
    )
    # check if we should save the model
    if i >= n_save_after:
        model.save("models/model_" + str(i) + ".h5")

# load models in order
members = load_all_models(5, 10)
print("Loaded %d models" % len(members))
# reverse loaded models so we build the ensemble with the last
models first
members = list(reversed(members))
```

```
# evaluate different numbers of ensembles on hold out set
single_scores, ensemble_scores = list(), list()
for i in range(1, len(members) + 1):
    # evaluate model with i members
    y_test_rounded = numpy.argmax(y_test, axis=1)
    ensemble_score = evaluate_n_members(members, i, x_test,
    y_test_rounded)
    # evaluate the i'th model standalone
    _, single_score = members[i - 1].evaluate(x_test, y_test,
    verbose=0)
    # print accuracy of single model vs ensemble output
    print("%d: single=%.3f, ensemble=%.3f" % (i, single_score,
    ensemble_score))
    ensemble_scores.append(ensemble_score)
    single_scores.append(single_score)
# Output:
# 1: single=0.731, ensemble=0.731
# 2: single=0.710, ensemble=0.728
# 3: single=0.712, ensemble=0.725
# 4: single=0.710, ensemble=0.727
# 5: single=0.696, ensemble=0.724
```

Snapshot Ensembles

Snapshot ensembles are an extension of a horizontal voting ensemble.
Instead of saving models after the minimum threshold, you modify the
learning rate of the model itself. If you have read or implemented deep
learning models, you may already know about this phenomenon. When
training a machine learning model, it is often desirable to start the initial
higher learning and then slowly decrease the learning rate.

In Figure 3-4, we are changing the learning rate with a training epoch. But oftentimes, this approach leaves a lot of the optimization on the table, as training could be struck at any local minimum.

One of the leading solutions for this local minimum problem is a **cyclic learning rate**, in which we increase and decrease learning rates in cycles.

Figure 3-4 shows that after each 400 epochs, we change the learning rate back to maximum value and then begin decreasing the learning rate from there.

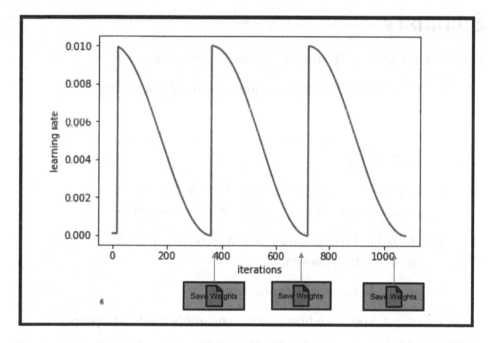

Figure 3-4. *Snapshot ensemble*

If you want to learn more about snapshot ensembles, refer to a Cornell University paper written in 2017 at https://arxiv.org/abs/1704.00109. In figure 1 of this paper, there is a loss vs. learning rate graph in standard SGD optimizer. It includes a simple learning rate schedule and a cyclic learning rate schedule. As a certain minimum is reached, we simply save the state of the model in the form of its weights and bias values obtained at that point and increase our learning rate (i.e., take a larger step). You can consider this larger step a jumping point for landing on a different spot in this plot and start finding the next minima. In the end, there are a set of models for which the error rate is low.

Like horizontal voting ensembles, all the models at each of the local minima states are combined. This approach results in a very good model when compared to using an individual model alone.

Summary

Let's do a quick recap of what you learned in this chapter.

- Ensemble learning techniques that involve a mixing models strategy

- Voting ensembles and its two variants: soft voting and hard voting

- Hyperparameter tuning ensembles, in which you combine models with different hyperparameters

- Horizontal voting ensembles, which are especially useful in deep learning

- Snapshot ensemble techniques

In Chapter 4, you learn how to build ensemble models by playing around with the mixing combinations strategy.

CHAPTER 4

Mixing Combinations

In the previous chapters, we discussed how to mix training data, as well as how to mix machine learning models to create more powerful models—leveraging the power of ensemble learning.

Let's continue this learning process. In this chapter, we introduce and explain two powerful ensemble learning techniques that leverage mixing combinations of machine learning models to make a more powerful model. We tackle different combinations one at a time.

The following are this chapter's goals.

- Introduce and explain **boosting**
- Examine how to implement boosting using scikit-learn
- Introduce and explain **stacking**
- Examine how to implement boosting using scikit-learn
- Look at other examples of mixing combinations

Boosting

Let's start the discussion of boosting by using an analogy of the learning process. Suppose you want a students in a class to perform well in all subjects, but some students performed poorly in unit tests. We can identify these students and provide more emphasis on the subjects in which they scored poorly so that they come up to par with other students. To provide more emphasis, we tweak the learning process by adding courses

© Alok Kumar and Mayank Jain 2020
A. Kumar and M. Jain, *Ensemble Learning for AI Developers*,
https://doi.org/10.1007/978-1-4842-5940-5_4

and allocating additional time to address the students' weak areas. This ensures that students perform better in all subjects overall.

Let's take this same analogy to machine learning. We start with a collection of learners. Each ML learner is trained on a particular subset of training objects. If a model learner has a weak performance, we could provide greater emphasis to that particular learner. This is known as **boosting**.

First, let's discuss one of the simplest but most important of boosting techniques, AdaBoost.

AdaBoost

To better understand AdaBoost, take a look at Figure 4-1. Initially data is trained using the Model classifier. The data subset in the red box is misclassified data; whereas the green box represents correctly classified data.

To improve the performance of the model, instead of giving equal weight to all data in the classifier model, we increase the weight of the incorrectly classified data and run the training again. Since we have increased the weight of incorrectly classified data points/observations, in the next iterations, they have a higher probability of correct classification because the model will give more importance to these data points. We repeat this process until n iterations, when we achieve our desired model performance. A combination of these weak classification learners uses voting (see Figure 4-2) to get the final model. Please note that this often outperforms very sophisticated techniques.

In summary, to increase efficiency, we can update the weight of incorrectly classified observations. Increasing the weight of incorrectly classified observations slightly helps improve the number of correctly classified observations in next iterations. By repeating these iterations, we can get a high-quality classifier from a very weak classifier. Even if we use a weakly performing machine learning model, we can boost output results.

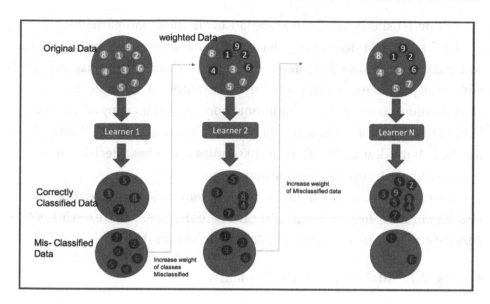

Figure 4-1. *AdaBoost boosting*

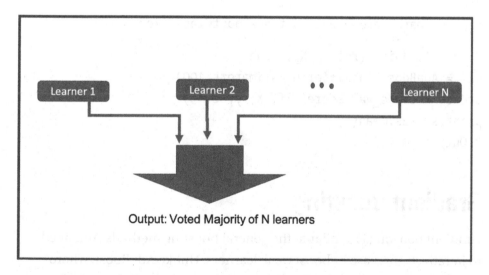

Figure 4-2. *Voting of n learners in AdaBoost boosting*

Listing 4-1 shows how to use AdaBoost with the scikit-learn library.

By default, scikit-learn uses a basic learner as a decision tree classifier with maximum depth = 1. To make an AdaBoost classifier, we pass an additional parameter, n_estimators (in this example, n_estimators = 100). AdaBoost is run on each additional boosted weight copy of the base learner until there is either a perfect data fit or the n_estimators limit is reached. At maximum, it will create 100 copies of our base decision tree learner with each copy having boosted weight.

You can read more about the different parameters for the AdaBoost classifier in scikit-learn at https://scikit-learn.org/stable/modules/generated/sklearn.ensemble.AdaBoostClassifier.html.

Listing 4-1. AdaBoost Using scikit-learn

```
from sklearn.model_selection import cross_val_score
from sklearn.datasets import load_iris
from sklearn.ensemble import AdaBoostClassifier

X, y = load_iris(return_X_y=True)
clf = AdaBoostClassifier(n_estimators=100)
scores = cross_val_score(clf, X, y, cv=5)
print(scores.mean())
# Output: 0.9466...
```

Gradient Boosting

Gradient boosting is similar to the general boosting methods. You need to iteratively increase or boost weak learners. Unlike AdaBoost, where you add a new learner after increasing the weight of badly classified observations, in gradient boosting, you train a new model on residual errors made by the previous predictor. If this doesn't make sense, don't worry. Let's look at an example.

First, try to understand the concept of residual errors. Figure 4-3 is an example dataset. X0 to X3 are the features/variables and Y is the ground truth, or target value.

Row Num	X0	X1	X2	X3	Y (Target Value)	Pred.	Error
0	0.94	0.27	0.80	0.34	1	0.80	0.20
1	0.84	0.79	0.89	0.05	1	0.75	0.25
2	0.83	0.11	0.23	0.42	1	0.65	0.35
3	0.74	0.26	0.03	0.41	0	0.40	-0.40
4	0.08	0.29	0.76	0.37	0	0.55	-0.55
5	0.71	0.76	0.43	0.95	1	0.34	0.66
6	0.08	0.72	0.97	0.04	0	0.02	-0.02

Figure 4-3. Residual errors

Now let's assume there is a trained a simple decision with very low depth (a weak learner) on this dataset. After training is completed, the predictions/inference on our decision tree is listed in the Pred column.

The difference between each output of each observation and predicted output from the machine learning model is called **residual error**. In Figure 4-3, the Error column represents the residual error field.

In a gradient-based boosting method, you learn a new classifier; instead of taking features X0 to X3, you take the residual error of the previous classifier as the new target (YNew) for training new models.

Let's summarize all the steps discussed so far.

1. Use a decision tree regressor on a training set.

2. Use a second decision tree regressor on the residual error of the first.

3. Use a third decision tree regressor on the residual error of the second.

You now have an ensemble containing three trees, and you can make predictions on new instances by summing up predictions from all the trees.

The output of this algorithm is shown in Figure 4-4.

Row Num	X0	X1	X2	X3	Y (old Target Value)	Old Pred.	Y New (new target value)	Pred
0	0.94	0.27	0.80	0.34	1	0.80	0.15	0.15
1	0.84	0.79	0.89	0.05	1	0.75	0.20	0.20
2	0.83	0.11	0.23	0.42	1	0.65	0.40	0.40
3	0.74	0.26	0.03	0.41	0	0.40	-0.30	-0.30
4	0.08	0.29	0.76	0.37	0	0.55	-0.20	-0.20
5	0.71	0.76	0.43	0.95	1	0.34	0.24	0.24
6	0.08	0.72	0.97	0.04	0	0.02	-0.01	-0.01

Y_Pred = Sum of all tree predictions

Figure 4-4. Residual error (continuation)

Listing 4-2 is example code for using gradient boosting in the scikit-learn library. By default, scikit-learn uses basic learner as decision tree classifier with maximum depth = 1.

You can read more about parameters for the gradient boosting classifier in scikit-learn at https://scikit-learn.org/stable/modules/generated/sklearn.ensemble.GradientBoostingClassifier.html.

Listing 4-2. Gradient Boosting with scikit-learn

```
from sklearn.datasets import make_hastie_10_2
from sklearn.ensemble import GradientBoostingClassifier
from sklearn.model_selection import cross_val_score

X, y = make_hastie_10_2(random_state=0)
clf = GradientBoostingClassifier(
    n_estimators=100, learning_rate=1.0, max_depth=1, random_
    state=0
).fit(X, y)

scores = cross_val_score(clf, X, y, cv=5)
print(scores.mean())
# Output: 0.9225
```

XGBoost

XGBoost is a state-of-the-art algorithm and software system specializing in residual gradient boosting techniques. It improves vanilla gradient boosting techniques by adding the following parameters (we which will not go into full detail).

- It dynamically determines the depth of decision trees used as weak learners, with penalization parameters added for prevention trees with high depth. This prevents overfitting and improves performance.

- It uses proportional shrinking of leaf nodes on the trees.

- It uses Newton's tree boosting for optimized learning of tree structures.

- It adds randomization parameters for optimal learning.

Listing 4-3 is example code for using XGBoost with the scikit-learn and XGBoost libraries.

Documentation on the XGBoost library is at `https://xgboost.readthedocs.io/en/latest/`.

The official GitHub page for XGBoost is at `https://github.com/dmlc/xgboost/`. There you find various code examples in classification and regression problems.

Tip   To easily install the XGBoost library in Anaconda Python version 3.7, use this command:conda install -c conda-forge xgboost

---

Listing 4-3. XGBoost Example on Breast Cancer Dataset Using scikit-learn and XGBoost Library

```
import xgboost as xgb
from sklearn.datasets import load_breast_cancer
from sklearn.model_selection import train_test_split
from sklearn.metrics import accuracy_score
import numpy as np
# read in data

iris = load_breast_cancer()
X = iris.data
y = iris.target

X_train, X_test, y_train, y_test = train_test_split(X, y,
test_size=0.2, random_state=42)

# use DMatrix for xgbosot
dtrain = xgb.DMatrix(X_train, label=y_train)
dtest = xgb.DMatrix(X_test, label=y_test)
```

```python
# set xgboost params
param = {
    'max_depth': 5,  # the maximum depth of each tree
    'eta': 0.3,  # the training step for each iteration
    'silent': 1,  # logging mode - quiet
    'objective': 'multi:softprob',  # error evaluation for
                                    multiclass training
    'num_class': 3}  # the number of classes that exist in this datset
num_round = 200  # the number of training iterations

bst = xgb.train(param, dtrain, num_round)
# make prediction
preds = bst.predict(dtest)
preds rounded = np.argmax(preds, axis=1)
print(accuracy_score(y_test, preds_rounded))
# Output: 0.9649122807017544
```

Stacking

Stacking is a slightly different way to mixing combinations.

In this ensemble technique we first train multiple models (**base learners**) together to get predictions. In stacking, the result of the individual predictions are then treated as next training data and added in form of another layer called **meta learner** (see Figure 4-5).

You can think of this technique as stacking one layer of machine learning learners on top of another machine learning learner.

Imagine that you are on a TV gameshow and must answer a history question. You ask for help from two of your friends; one is a history major and the other is computer science major. Who would you trust more to have the correct answer? Your knowledge enables you to trust your history friend's answer more (or technically speaking, to give higher value to one of the underlying learners).

Stacking is based on the same idea: instead of using trivial functions (such as hard voting) to aggregate the predictions of all learners in an ensemble, we train a model to perform this aggregation. Let's look at an example to understand this better.

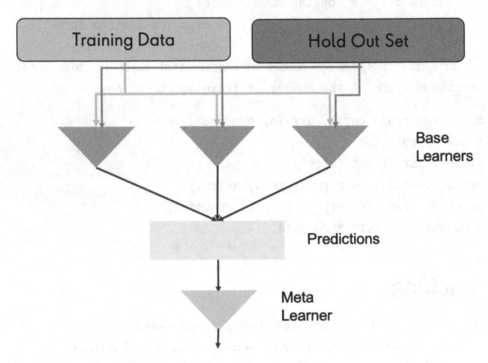

Figure 4-5. Stacking

Listing 4-4 is example code for using stacking in the scikit-learn library. Also if you want to apply stacking to any regression problem you can take help of Listing 4-5 where we have used stacking using scikit learn library on a regression problem.

You can read more about different parameters for the Stacking classifier in scikit-learn from the reference page at https://scikit-learn.org/stable/ modules/generated/sklearn.ensemble.StackingClassifier.html.

Listing 4-4. Stacking Classifier Using scikit-learn

```
from sklearn.datasets import load_iris
from sklearn.ensemble import RandomForestClassifier
from sklearn.svm import LinearSVC
from sklearn.linear_model import LogisticRegression
from sklearn.preprocessing import StandardScaler
from sklearn.pipeline import make_pipeline
from sklearn.ensemble import StackingClassifier

X, y = load_iris(return_X_y=True)
estimators = [
    ("rf", RandomForestClassifier(n_estimators=10, random_
    state=42)),
    ("svr", make_pipeline(StandardScaler(), LinearSVC(random_
    state=42))),
]
clf = StackingClassifier(estimators=estimators, final_estimator=
LogisticRegression())

from sklearn.model_selection import train_test_split

X_train, X_test, y_train, y_test = train_test_split(X, y,
stratify=y, random_state=42)
clf.fit(X_train, y_train).score(X_test, y_test)
# Output: 0.9...
```

Listing 4-5. Stacking Regression Using scikit-learn

```
from sklearn.datasets import load_diabetes
from sklearn.linear_model import RidgeCV
from sklearn.svm import LinearSVR
from sklearn.ensemble import RandomForestRegressor
from sklearn.ensemble import StackingRegressor
```

```
X, y = load_diabetes(return_X_y=True)
estimators = [("lr", RidgeCV()), ("svr", LinearSVR(random_
state=42))]
reg = StackingRegressor(
    estimators=estimators,
    final_estimator=RandomForestRegressor(n_estimators=10,
    random_state=42),
)
from sklearn.model_selection import train_test_split

X_train, X_test, y_train, y_test = train_test_split(X, y,
random_state=42)
reg.fit(X_train, y_train).score(X_test, y_test)
# Output: 0.3...
```

Summary

Let's do a quick recap of what was covered in this chapter.

- Combining ensembles

- Important combination techniques: boosting and stacking

- Various boosting techniques, including AdaBoost, gradient boosting, and XGBoost

- Stacking adds one set of ensemble learners on top of others to make a metalearner

- Stacking in classification and regression problems with code examples in scikit-learn

CHAPTER 5

Using Ensemble Learning Libraries

The use of high-quality libraries speeds initial development, results in fewer bugs, reduces reinvention-of-the-wheel scenarios, and cuts long-term maintenance costs. Given that machine learning is inherently experimental in nature, libraries enable fast and maintainable experiments.

The goals of this chapter are to

- Introduce ML-Ensemble, a Python-based open source library that wraps scikit ensemble classes to offer a high-level API.

- Scale XGBoost via Dask, a flexible library for parallel computing in Python. Dask and XGBoost can work together to train gradient-boosted trees in parallel.

- Learn boosting using Microsoft LightGBM.

- Introduce AdaNet, a lightweight TensorFlow-based framework for learning neural network architecture, but is also used for learning to ensemble models.

© Alok Kumar and Mayank Jain 2020
A. Kumar and M. Jain, *Ensemble Learning for AI Developers*,
https://doi.org/10.1007/978-1-4842-5940-5_5

ML-Ensemble

ML-Ensemble, also known as mlens, is an open source Python library for building scikit-learn-compatible ensemble estimators.

You can install it via pip.

```
pip install mlens
```

The API style to build the ensembles is very similar to libraries like Keras. It offers a very simple and straightforward way to build deep ensembles with complex interactions.

But, why do we need a separate library for ensembling? Well, scikit-learn does not support stacking directly. You can still write it, but then you will have to maintain it yourself. ML-Ensemble offers a generic way to ensemble estimators and has reasonable documentation. It is worth exploring, even if you decide to not use it in production code. The API helps you experiment with different ensembles very quickly.

Let's build a stacked ensemble via mlens. Recall that **stacking** combines multiple classification or regression estimators via a metalearner. The first-level estimators are trained based on a complete training set, and then the metalearner is trained on the output of the first-layer estimators' predictions.

Let's set up the data first. We will use the make_moons dataset. In case you don't know, make_moons is a simple toy dataset that makes two half interleaving circles.

Listing 5-1. Stacked ensemble via mlens

```
# ---Data setup----
import numpy as np
from sklearn.metrics import accuracy_score
from sklearn.datasets import make_moons
seed = 42
```

```
X, y = make_moons(n_samples=10000,noise=0.4, random_state=seed)
# --- 1. Initialize ---
from mlens.ensemble import SuperLearner
ensemble = SuperLearner(scorer=accuracy_score, random_
state=seed)
# --- 2. Build the first layer ---
ensemble.add([RandomForestClassifier(random_state=seed),
SVC(random_state=seed)])
# --- 3. Attach the final meta learner ---
ensemble.add_meta(LogisticRegression())
# --- Train ---
ensemble.fit(X_train, y_train)
# --- Predict ---
preds  ensemble.predict(X test)
```

Now, let's go through the code. The ensembling is essentially a three-step process.

1. Initialize the ensemble, which is SuperLearner here.

2. Add the intermediate estimators. Here we are adding two classifiers: RandomForest and SVM. Note that they will execute in parallel.

3. Add the metalearner, which is LogisticRegression here.

4. Call the fit method and do the predictions. Visually, it can be represented as shown in Figure 5-1.

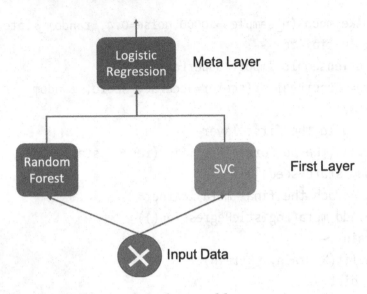

Figure 5-1. *Single layer stacked ensemble*

Doesn't it feel like setting up a neural network where we stack layers to build the network?

To check the performance of the estimator in the layers, call the data attribute.

```
print("Fit data:\n%r" % ensemble.data)
```

Fit data:

		score-m	score-s	ft-m	ft-s	pt-m	pt-s
layer-1	randomforestclassifier	0.84	0.00	0.06	0.00	0.01	0.00
layer-1	svc	0.86	0.00	0.14	0.00	0.06	0.00

The first column, score-m, contains the score. The suffix -m denotes mean values, and -s denotes standard deviation across folds for brevity. ft and pt stand for fit time and prediction time, respectively. We encourage you to read the documents for further information. Note that we provided the scoring function during superlearner initialization. If we can add two estimators at the first layer, then it should not be a surprise that you can add more estimators at any layer.

Multilayer Ensembles

Adding multiple layers is equally straightforward. We just need to call the add function to add a new layer. Note that layers are executed in sequence. However, within a layer, estimators can run parallel.

```
ensemble = SuperLearner(scorer=accuracy_score, random_
state=seed, verbose=2)

# Build the first layer
ensemble.add([RandomForestClassifier(random_state=seed),
LogisticRegression(random_state=seed)])

# Build the 2nd layer
ensemble.add([LogisticRegression(random_state=seed),
SVC(random_state=seed)])

# Attach the final meta estimator
ensemble.add_meta(SVC(random_state=seed))
```

Figure 5-2 is a visual representation of the ensemble.

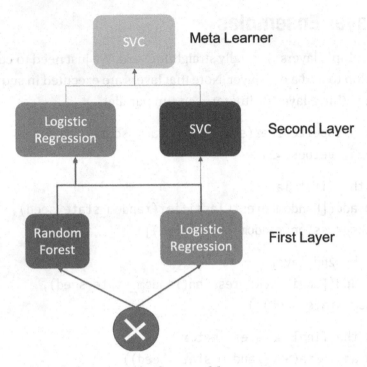

Figure 5-2. Multilayer stacked ensemble

Ensemble Model Selection

To fully exploit the learning capacity in an ensemble, it is important to conduct hyperparameter tuning, treating the base learner's parameters as the parameters of the ensemble. Metalearner is the critical part of the ensemble, but how would you select an appropriate metalearner? The task of selecting the appropriate metalearner becomes computationally intensive if the entire ensemble has to be evaluated each time.

One possible workaround for this problem is to treat the lower layers of an ensemble as a preprocessing pipeline, and then only performing model selection on higher-order layers or metalearners. Think of preprocessing pipelines as cached results that are evaluated only once. To use an ensemble for this purpose, set the model_selection parameter to True before fitting. This will modify how the transform method behaves and ensure that predict is called on test folds.

Before we look at the end-to-end code for model selection, there are few more library pieces that you need to understand.

The Scoring Function

We need to wrap the scoring function inside the mlens **make_scorer()** function.

This essentially makes a scorer from a performance metric or loss function.

```
from mlens.metrics import make_scorer
accuracy_scorer = make_scorer(accuracy_score, greater_is_
better=True)
```

The true value of the greater_is_better parameter indicates accuracy, whereas False indicates error/loss.

But why do we need to do it? This is required to ensure that all learners scoring is done in the same way.

The make_scorer wrapper is a copy of scikit-learn's **sklearn. metrics.make_scorer()**. sklearn make_scorer is a factory function that wraps scoring functions for use in GridSearchCV and cross_val_score. It takes a score function, such as **accuracy_score, mean_squared_error**, **adjusted_rand_index**, or **average_precision** and returns a callable that scores an estimator's output. So that you are not lost here, remember that our objective is to find the appropriate metalearners. Now that you know how to make scoring consistent, let's discuss how the library manages the processing pipeline.

Evaluator

The mlens Evaluator class allows you to grid search several models in parallel across several preprocessing pipelines. The evaluator class prefits transformers, thus avoiding fitting the same preprocessing pipelines on the same data repeatedly. Let's go through the code to understand it better. We have skipped some of the common and obvious code for brevity.

```
from mlens.model_selection import Evaluator
from scipy.stats import randint
from sklearn.naive_bayes import GaussianNB
from sklearn.neighbors import KNeighborsClassifier
```

Now we need to name the estimators.

```
ests = [('gnb', GaussianNB()), ('knn', KNeighborsClassifier())]
```

Then we prepare the parameters list. This is no different from what you do during a grid or random search. Note that GNB is not included because it doesn't have any parameters.

```
pars = {'n_neighbors': randint(2, 20)}
params = {'knn': pars}
```

We can now run an evaluation over these estimators and parameter distributions by calling the evaluate method.

```
evaluator = Evaluator(scorer=accuracy_scorer, cv=10)
evaluator.fit(X, y, ests, params, n_iter=10)
```

You can check the results and summary via Evaluator's cv_results and summary properties.

Preprocessing

The mlens preprocessing feature helps you compare the models across a set of preprocessing pipelines. It does this via a class that acts as a transformer, allowing you to use lower or incoming layers as a "preprocessing" step, so that you need only evaluate the metalearners iteratively. Let's look at the code to understand it better.

```
from sklearn.preprocessing import StandardScaler
preprocess_cases = {'none': [],
                    'sc': [StandardScaler()]
                    }
```

We have specified a dictionary of preprocessing pipelines to run through. Each entry in the dictionary is a list of transformers to apply sequentially.

It's now time to look at an end-to-end example to see all the pieces in action.

Listing 5-2. Processing pipeline via mlens

```
from mlens.model_selection import Evaluator
from mlens.ensemble import SequentialEnsemble #--1
from mlens.metrics import make_scorer
from scipy.stats import uniform, randint

base_learners = [RandomForestClassifier(random_state=seed),
                 SVC(probability=True)] #--2

proba_transformer = SequentialEnsemble(
                model_selection=True, random_state=seed).add(
                'blend', base_learners, proba=True) #--3
class_transformer = SequentialEnsemble(
                model_selection=True, random_state=seed).add(
                'blend', base_learners, proba=False) #--4
```

```
preprocessing = {'proba': [('layer-1', proba_transformer)],
                 'class': [('layer-1', class_transformer)]} #--5

meta_learners = [SVC(random_state=seed), ('rf',
RandomForestClassifier(random_state=seed))] #--6
params = {'svc': {'C': uniform(0, 10)},
          'class.rf': {'max_depth': randint(2, 10)},
          'proba.rf': {'max_depth': randint(2, 10),
                       'max_features': uniform(0.5, 0.5)}
          } #--7
scorer = make_scorer(accuracy_score) #--8
evaluator = Evaluator(scorer=scorer, random_state=seed, cv=2) #--9

evaluator.fit(X, y, meta_learners, params,
preprocessing=preprocessing, n_iter=2)#--10
from pandas import DataFrame
df = DataFrame(evaluator.results) #--11
```

	test_score-m	test_score-s	train_score-m	train_score-s	fit_time-m	fit_time-s	pred_time-m	pred_time-s	params
class.rf	0.8621	0.0019	0.8588	0.0008	1.773437	0.079849	0.361450	0.045035	{'max_depth': 8}
class.svc	0.8621	0.0019	0.8588	0.0008	1.141838	0.028914	0.091293	0.057192	{'C': 3.745401188473625}
proba.rf	0.8575	0.0019	0.8752	0.0056	1.683211	0.063803	0.253456	0.107526	{'max_depth': 5, 'max_features': 0.97535715320...
proba.svc	0.8618	0.0004	0.8588	0.0020	0.689784	0.041124	0.062543	0.034615	{'C': 3.745401188473625}

Let's unpack the code.

1. Import the **SequentialEnsemble** class. The
    SequentialEnsemble allows users to build ensembles
    with different classes of layers. The classes of layers
    are blend, subset, and stack. These three classes are
    different ways of mapping a training set to a prediction
    set used by the metalearner.

2. Use RandomForest and SVM as the base learners.

3. Set up two competing ensemble bases as preprocessing transformers. This one is a blended ensemble base with proba. Note that proba means whether the layer should predict class probabilities. Here the estimators' **predict_proba** method will be called.

4. This one is a blended ensemble without proba. Note that the model_selection parameter is set to True. This modifies how the transform method behaves and ensures predict is called on test folds.

5. Set up preprocessing mapping. Each pipeline in this map is fitted once on each fold before evaluating candidate metalearners.

6. Set up candidate metalearners. Here the estimators will run on all preprocessing pipelines.

7. Set up parameter mappings. Note that the distributions are differentiated between cases for the random forest.

8. Wrap the score function. You already know why.

9. Instantiate the evaluator.

10. Call the evaluator fit method.

11. This is not required, but you can load the evaluator result in a dataframe to view the results in a formatted way. Again, the -s and -m suffixes stand for mean and standard deviation, respectively.

> ❶ Warning
>
> Remember to turn model selection off when done.

Summary

Let's do a quick recap. ML-Ensemble offers Keras-style API build ensembles. The superlearner class helps with building stacking ensembles. mlens offers different kinds of stacking layers, such as stack, blend, and subset. Running an entire ensemble several times to compare different metalearners can be prohibitively expensive. ML-Ensemble implements a class that acts as a transformer, allowing you to use ingoing layers as a "preprocessing" step, so that you need only to evaluate the metalearners iteratively. You can find the project documentation at `http://ml-ensemble.com/info/index.html`.

Scale XGBoost via Dask

As you already know, XGBoost is an optimized implementation of gradient boosting, whereas Dask is a flexible library for parallel computing in Python.

You can combine the two to train gradient-boosted trees in parallel.

Before we scale XGBoost via Dask, you need to understand Dask.

To understand and appreciate the value of Dask, you need to look at the Python scientific ecosystem. Figure 5-3 gives you a general idea of the broad availability of so many useful libraries and frameworks.

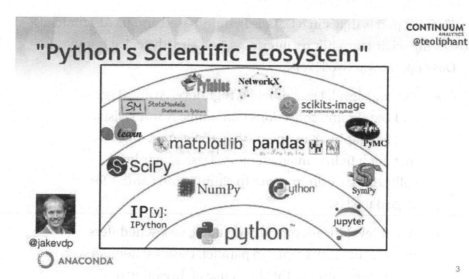

Figure 5-3. *Python's Scientific Ecosystem*

However, these packages were not designed to scale beyond a single machine. Dask was developed to scale these packages and the surrounding ecosystem. It works with the existing Python ecosystem to scale it to multicore machines and distributed clusters. Most of these libraries are not scalable. How would you use NumPy or Pandas for datasets that won't fit in your computer memory? Dask makes NumPy and Pandas work with distributed data. Isn't the idea of distributed NumPy and Pandas cool and exciting? Dask isn't restricted to scaling NumPy and Pandas, though; the scalability benefit is extended to the whole ecosystem.

At a high level, Dask helps you solve two problems.

- Handling datasets that are larger than RAM. (You already know that Pandas and NumPy require the full dataset in memory.)

- Distributing a task across threads, cores, or different machines.

The best part is that since Dask is Python-based and its API matches most of the scikit-learn library interfaces, you already feel at home.

Dask operates at two levels.

- At a high level, Dask provides high-level Array, Bag, and DataFrame collections that mimic NumPy, lists, and Pandas but can operate in parallel on datasets that don't fit into main memory. Dask's high-level collections are alternatives to NumPy and Pandas for large datasets.

- At low levels, Dask provides dynamic task schedulers that execute task graphs in parallel. Dask's schedulers are an alternative to the direct use of threading or multiprocessing libraries in complex cases or other task scheduling systems, like Luigi or IPython Parallel.

A logical architecture of Dask (see Figure 5-4) can help you understand the concepts better.

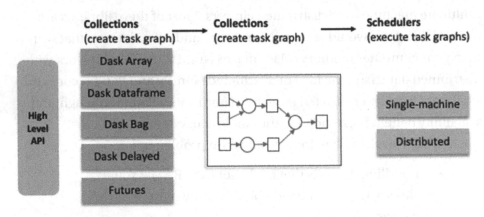

Figure 5-4. *Dask architecture*

Let's now look under the hood to learn about the Dask arrays and dataframes.

Dask Arrays and Dataframes

A picture speaks a thousand words. A logical structure of the Dask array is shown in Figure 5-5.

Figure 5-5. Logical structure of Dask array

You can see in Figure 5-5 that the Dask array essentially manages the collection of NumPy arrays, even though it gives a single logical view to the user. This picture might trigger ideas in your mind, and yes, they are true. You can assign individual NumPy arrays that process to different threads, cores, or machines. It doesn't matter where they live. Dask is a wonderful secretary that manages all the coordination internally.

The same picture (see Figure 5-6) can be used for dataframes as well. Dask dataframes coordinate many Pandas dataframes, partitioned along an index.

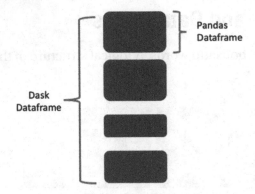

Figure 5-6. *Logical structure of a Dask dataframe*

Let's look at the code to see how to read a CSV in a Dask dataframe.

```
import dask.dataframe as dd
df = pd.read_csv("hdfs://mycsv.csv", parse_dates
=['timestamp'])
```

Let's also look at how it would have been done in Pandas.

```
import pandas as pd
df = dd.read_csv("hdfs://mycsv.csv", parse_dates
=['timestamp'])
```

The code is identical across two libraries, and this is not a copy/paste error. The Dask API was designed keeping Python style in mind to ensure that the learning curve is minimal. Almost all packages in the Python data computing ecosystem can derive the benefits of distributed and parallel processing without much change.

In addition to distributed processing, parallel processing is another Dask feature to scale data processing tasks. Let's look at how Dask can parallelize custom algorithms using the simpler dask.delayed interface. Let's go through the code in Listing 5-3.

Listing 5-3. Dask delayed interface for parallel processing

```python
def inc(x):
    return x + 1
def double(x):
    return x * 2
def add(x, y):
    return x + y

data = [1, 2, 3, 4, 5]

output = []

for x in data:
    a = inc(x)
    b = double(x)
    c = add(a, b)
    output.append(c)
total = sum(output)
```

Although the code is trivial, you can clearly see that the processing can be parallelized. inc and double can be executed in parallel.

The Dask delayed function can decorate the preceding functions so that they operate *lazily*. Rather than executing the function immediately, it defers execution, placing the function and its arguments into a task graph. Let's now wrap the custom functions within the delayed function, as shown in Listing 5-4.

Listing 5-4. Dask lazy execution

```python
import dask
output = []
for x in data:
    a = dask.delayed(inc)(x)
    b = dask.delayed(double)(x)
```

```
    c = dask.delayed(add)(a, b)
    output.append(c)
total = dask.delayed(sum)(output)
```

It is important to note that None of the inc, double, add, or sum calls have happened yet. Instead, the object total is a delayed result that contains a task graph of the entire computation.

Fortunately, you can view the task graph by calling the total. visualize() method, as shown in Figure 5-7.

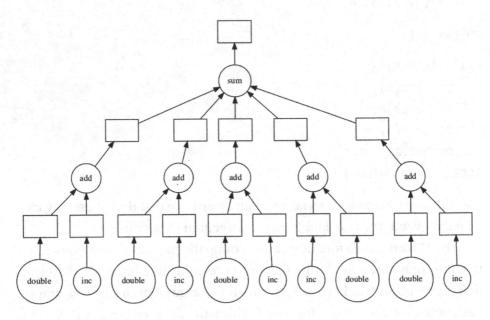

Figure 5-7. *Dask tasks graph*

Each of the nodes in the graph are tasks that can be assigned to different threads, pools, or even machines. The nodes are executed when the operation is run. For the code in Listing 5-2, it would be a call to the compute function.

```
total.compute()
```

It is important to be clear on what is happening here. It is not a large dataset problem but a computation challenge. When you hear about "messy data," the majority of the time, it is a combination of a large dataset and custom data processing logic. Dask operates at both levels: large data and parallelizing tasks in an execution. Listing 5-5 is the graph of the Dask array task.

Listing 5-5. Dask task graph

```
import dask.array as da
x = da.ones((15, 15), chunks=(5, 5))
y = x + x.T
y.visualize()
```

Here we are creating a Dask 2D array made from three chunks of a shape (5,5) and then adding the array with its transpose. Figure 5-8 is the task graph for the computation.

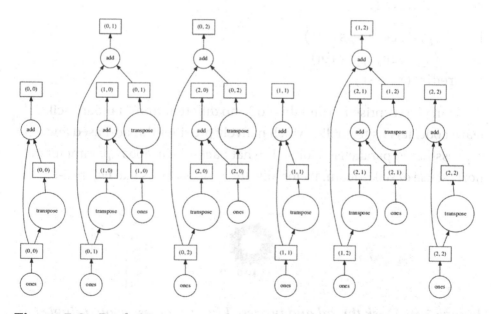

Figure 5-8. *Dask 2D arrays tasks graph*

Dask-ML

What would you get if you combine Dask with scikit-learn? You get a scalable ML algorithm.

But isn't scikit-learn already parallel? Yes, but scikit-learn only provides parallel computing on a single machine with Joblib. Let's build a classifier using LogisticRegression (see Listing 5-6). We will use the make_classification dataset that generates a random n classification problem.

Listing 5-6. Single Machine logisticRegression with Dask

```
from dask_glm.datasets import make_classification
from dask_ml.linear_model import LogisticRegression
from dask_ml.model_selection import train_test_split

X, y = make_classification()
X_train, X_test, y_train, y_test = train_test_split(X, y,
random_state=42)

lr = LogisticRegression()
lr.fit(X_train, y_train)
lr.predict(X_test)
```

Don't be surprised to find this code no different from standard scikit-learn code. It is using Joblib, which natively provides thread-based and process-based parallelism. Joblib is what backs the n_jobs= parameter in normal use of scikit-learn. Pictorially, the process looks like Figure 5-9.

Figure 5-9. *Dask thread and process-based processing on a single machine using Joblib*

Note   Please check documentation for installing dask_ml.

Dask can extend this parallelism to many machines in a cluster. This works well for modest data sizes, but large computations, such as random forests, hyperparameter optimization, and more. Before we look at the code, Figure 5-10 shows what the distributed computation looks like.

Figure 5-10. *Dask parallel execution in a clustered environment*

Here, Dask is talking to scikit-learn via Joblib so that a cluster is used to train a model. Let's go through the code in Listing 5-7 to see things in action.

Listing 5-7. GridSearch and LogisticRegression via dask

```
from dask_ml.model_selection import GridSearchCV
parameters = {'penalty': ['l1', 'l2'], 'C': [0.5, 1, 2]}
lr = LogisticRegression()
est = GridSearchCV(lr, param_grid=parameters)
est.fit(X_train,y_train)
```

No surprises until now. We are using the grid search to find the best value for logisticRegression parameters: penalty and coefficient C. The dataset is the same as the one we used in Listing 5-6. Now we want to switch the training on a cluster.

Listing 5-8. Training on a cluster via dask

```
from dask_ml.model_selection import GridSearchCV

parameters = {'penalty': ['l1', 'l2'], 'C': [0.5, 1, 2]}

lr = LogisticRegression()
est = GridSearchCV(lr, param_grid=parameters)

import joblib #--1
from dask.distributed import Client #--2

client = Client() #--3

with joblib.parallel_backend('dask'): #--4
    est.fit(X_train, y_train) #--5
```

Let's unpack the code. Note that there is no change in scikit-learn grid search code and we are using the same data as in Listing 5-6.

1. We import the Joblib library. Recall that Joblib runs the scikit-sklearn function on different threads or processes on a local machine. We are importing this to register the new back end, which is Dask here. It is essentially to change from Figure 5-9 to Figure 5-10.

2. We import the **Client** from Dask **dask.distributed** to connect to the Dask cluster.

3. We are initializing the client to connect to the Dask cluster. But when did we start the cluster? The cluster is run locally when the client is initialized with no parameter. To run the cluster locally, all we need to do is initialize the **Client** without any parameter.

4. With the **joblib.parallel_backend** context, we are specifying to use the Dask back end or cluster for training.

5. Now the estimator is fit onto the cluster rather than on threads or processes.

The cluster could be run in a cloud environment with Docker or Kubernetes. Please check the documentation for setting up clusters on cloud machines.

Scaling XGBoost

You learned about XGBoost in previous chapters. Here you learn how to train gradient boosting trees in parallel using Dask and XGBoost. Recall that XGBoost stands for eXtreme Gradient Boosting, and as the name suggests, it is an implementation of gradient boosting. The gradient boosting method tries to fit a new predictor to the *residual errors* made by the previous predictor.

The **dask-xgboost** project is pretty small and pretty simple (200 TLOC). Like a Dask cluster that has scheduler(s) and worker(s), Dask starts up an XGBoost scheduler in the same process running the Dask scheduler and an XGBoost worker within each of the Dask workers. They share the same physical processes and memory spaces. Dask is built to support this kind of situation, which is why it is so seamless. During training, Dask workers give all the Pandas dataframes (that are constituents of the Dask dataframe) to the local XGBoost and let XGBoost do its thing. It is important to note and remember that Dask doesn't power XGBoost; it just sets it up, gives it data, and lets it do its work in the background.

Dask and XGBoost can share data with each other and can monitor each other because they can live in the same Python process. It is very similar to the way NumPy and Pandas operate together within a single process. Sharing distributed processes with multiple systems can be really beneficial if you want to use multiple specialized services easily and avoid large monolithic frameworks. Let's now look at how to use XGBoost with Dask in code (see Listing 5-9).

Listing 5-9. Scaling XGBoost via dask

```
from dask.distributed import Client
client = Client() # --1
#Prepare dummy dataset
from dask_ml.datasets import make_classification
X, y = make_classification(n_samples=100000, n_features=20,
                            chunks=1000, n_informative=4,
                            random_state=0) #--2

#Split for training and testing
from dask_ml.model_selection import train_test_split
X_train, X_test, y_train, y_test = train_test_split(X, y,
test_size=0.15) #--3

#Train Dask-XGBoost
import xgboost
import dask_xgboost

params = {'objective': 'binary:logistic',
          'max_depth': 4, 'eta': 0.01, 'subsample': 0.5,
          'min_child_weight': 0.5} #--4

bst = dask_xgboost.train(client, params, X_train, y_train,
                          num_boost_round=10) #--5

#Plot feature importance
%matplotlib inline
import matplotlib.pyplot as plt
```

```
ax = xgboost.plot_importance(bst, height=0.8, max_num_
features=9)
ax.grid(False, axis="y")
ax.set_title('Estimated feature importance')
plt.show()

#Results
```

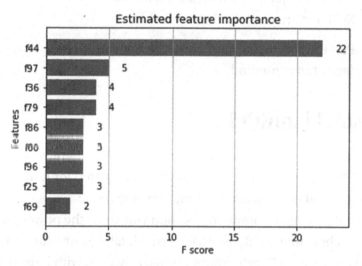

Figure 5-11. *Feature importance score plot*

Let's unpack the code here.

1. Initialize the client. You already know that Dask
    cluster will be a local one. You can check the value
    of cluster to see the cluster details.

2. Generate a random toy dataset using the make_
    classification function. We have used this before as
    well.

3. Split THE dataset into training and testing data to
    aid evaluation by making sure we have a fair test.

4. Specify the XGBoost parameters.

5. Call the train method to fit the model. dask-xgboost
    is a small wrapper around XGBoost. Dask sets up
    XGBoost, gives XGBoost data, and lets XGBoost
    do its training in the background using all the
    Dask workers. The bst object is a regular xgboost.
    Booster object, which means all the methods of
    XGBoost are available here.

6. Plot the feature importance using xgboost.plot_
    importance method.

Microsoft LightGBM

LightGBM is a fast, distributed, high-performance gradient boosting
framework based on decision tree algorithms. It is used for ranking,
classification, and many other machine learning tasks.

If you follow Kaggle competitions, then you know the power and
popularity of boosting. XGBoost, that started it all, became the standard
algorithm for winning Kaggle competitions. However, with large data,
the training time with XGBoost goes up drastically. LightGBM addresses
the problem of scalability and speed, with significantly lower memory
consumption. It is worthwhile to remember that both XGBoost and
LightGBM are specific instances of GBT (gradient boosting), and they both
implement the same underlying algorithm; however, they each introduce
various tricks to make training more efficient or to improve performance. It
is designed to be distributed and efficient with the following advantages.

- Faster training speed and higher efficiency

- Lower memory usage

- Better accuracy

- Support for parallel and GPU learning

- Capable of handling large-scale data

Why LightGBM Architecture Is Best

XGBoost and LightGBM, being part of the same gradient boosted decision trees (GBDT) family, have a similar architecture. Here, we focus on architecture ideas that make LightGBM train accurate models.

Growing the Tree

In order to split and train each individual decision tree, there are two strategies that can be employed: level-wise and leaf-wise.

The level-wise strategy maintains a balanced tree. A balanced tree is a tree where every leaf is "not more than a certain distance" away from the root than any other leaf. Essentially, all the leaf nodes are at the same distance from the root. You can see in Figure 5-12 that the splits are ensuring that the tree maintains the balance.

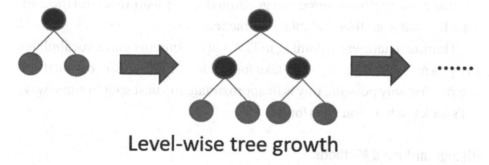

Level-wise tree growth

Figure 5-12. Level-wise tree split strategy (Source: https://mlexplained.com)

The leaf-wise strategy splits the leaf that reduces the loss the most (see Figure 5-13). This makes the training flexible, although susceptible to overfitting. LightGBM grows trees leaf-wise. It chooses the leaf with maximum delta loss to grow. By holding the number of leaves fixed, leaf-wise algorithms tend to achieve a lower loss than level-wise algorithms. It is interesting to note that leaf-wise growth was an exclusive feature of LightGBM, but XGBoost has also implemented this growth strategy.

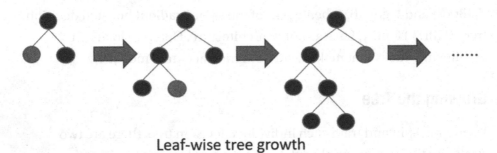

Leaf-wise tree growth

Figure 5-13. *Leaf-wise tree split strategy (Source: https://mlexplained.com)*

Finding the Best Split

Finding the best split for each leaf is a key challenge in training GBDT.

You could use brute force and go through every feature to find the best split, but that is neither scalable nor practical.

Think of a dataset containing millions of documents and a vocabulary size of a million words. It would take forever for GBDT to train on the tf-idf matrix. The only possible way is to approximate the best split in some way. Let's look at a few strategies for this.

Histogram-based Methods

Histogram-based methods group features into a set of bins and perform splitting on the bins instead of the features. This helps speed up the training and reduce the complexity, as the features can be binned before building each tree. Note that the features must be sorted in advance for this method to be effective.

Treating Missing Values

The input to LightGBM tends to be sparse given the fact that it is used a lot on tabular or text data. One possible option is to ignore the missing value and then assign it to any side of the split that reduces the loss. This is what LightGBM does when the `zero_as_missing` parameter is set to `True`. It regards all zero values as missing.

Gradient-based One-Side Sampling

It is a common observation that not all features play an important role in training. Such features have a lower gradient. LightGBM concentrates on data points with high gradients (i.e., during the best split, it tends to ignore low-gradient features). However, this comes with the inherent risk of biased sampling. In order to mitigate these problems, LightGBM applies two tricks: randomly sample data with smaller gradients and importance sampling. This essentially increases the weight of the samples with small gradients while computing their contributions to the change in loss.

Exclusive Feature Bundling

Exclusive feature bundling is a technique to leverage the sparsity of the large datasets. Given the sparsity, some features are never non-zero together; for example, Python and politics have very few chances of coming together in a document. They can be "bundled" into a single feature without losing any information. Finding the best bundle is an NP-hard problem, and hence, LightGBM uses an approximation technique that tolerates a certain degree of overlap between the non-zero elements within a feature bundle. Going into the details of that approximation does not have much value here, but if you are interested, you can read the full paper at `www.microsoft.com/en-us/research/wp-content/uploads/2017/11/lightgbm.pdf`.

Now that you know more about the workings of LightGBM, understanding its parameters should be easy.

Parameters

As no surprise, the parameters format is key1=value1 key2=value2 .....
It can be set both in the config file and the command line. By using the
command line, parameters should not have spaces before and after =. By
using config files, one line can only contain one parameter. You can use #
to comment.

If one parameter appears in both the command line and the config
file, LightGBM will use the parameter from the command line. Rather
than listing the parameters here, read the documentation at https://
lightgbm.readthedocs.io/en/latest/Parameters.html.

LightGBM in Python Code

Let's build a binary classifier using LightGBM. We will use the Python
interface for the use case (see Listing 5-10).

Listing 5-10. Binary Classifier using lightGBM

```
import lightgbm as lgb # --1
n_features  = 20
data = np.random.rand(5000, 20)  # --2
label = np.random.randint(2, size=5000)
X_trn, X_val, y_trn, y_val = train_test_split(data, label,
test_size=0.30)  # --3
feature_name = ['feature_' + str(col) for col in range
(n_features)] # --4
train_data = lgb.Dataset(X_trn,label=y_trn,feature_
name=feature_name, categorical_feature=[feature_name[-1]] #--5
validation_data = lgb.Dataset(X_val,label=y_
val,reference=train_data) # --6
param = {'num_leaves': 31, 'objective': 'binary'} # --7
param['metric'] = ['auc', 'binary_logloss'] # --8
```

```
num_round = 10
bst = lgb.train(param, train_data, num_round, valid_
sets=[validation_data]) #--9
print('Feature importances:', list(bst.feature_importance()))
# --10
data = np.random.rand(7, 20)
ypred = bst.predict(data) # --11
# --12
for i in range(7):
    if ypred[i]>=.5:          # setting threshold to .5
        ypred[i]=1
    else:
        ypred[i]=0
```

Let's unpack the code.

1. Import the LightGBM library. Other imports have been omitted for brevity.

   The LightGBM Python module can load data from a LibSVM (zero-based) /TSV/CSV/ TXT format file, a NumPy 2D array(s), a Pandas dataframe, an H2O DataTable's frame, and a SciPy sparse matrix LightGBM binary file. The data is stored in a Dataset object.

2. Split the data into train and validation.

3. Assign names to the randomly generated features. Note that we have 20 features in our dataset.

4. Prepare the training dataset. We are specifying the features names and categorical values. LightGBM can use categorical features as input directly. It doesn't need to convert to one-hot coding, and it is

much faster than one-hot coding (about 8x speed-up). It is important to convert categorical values to int before loading into datasets.

5. Prepare the validation dataset. In LightGBM, the validation data should be aligned with training data. The Dataset object here is very memory-efficient, and it only needs to save discrete bins.

6. LightGBM can use a dictionary to set Parameters. Since this is a binary classification problem, we are setting up the objective as binary. Check the documentation for other possible values for objective.

7. Specify multiple eval metrics.

8. Train by calling the train method. You can also use fit and check the documentation for details.

9. Check the feature importance by using the feature_importance method.

10. Call the predict method to calculate the class probabilities.

11. Convert the probabilities into class predictions using a threshold.

There is one more area of parameter tuning, and for that we recommend going through the documentation at https://lightgbm.readthedocs.io/en/latest/Parameters-Tuning.html. With your new knowledge of architecture, it won't be difficult to understand.

AdaNet

AdaNet is a lightweight TensorFlow-based framework for automatically learning high-quality models with minimal expert intervention. It is an algorithm for iteratively learning both the **structure** and **weight** of a neural network as an **ensemble of subnetworks**.

This project is based on the AdaNet algorithm, presented in "AdaNet: Adaptive Structural Learning of Artificial Neural Networks" at ICML 2017, for learning the structure of a neural network as an ensemble of subnetworks.

A picture is helpful here (see Figure 5-14).

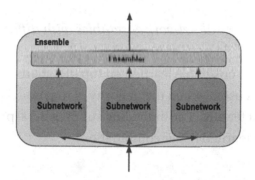

Figure 5-14. *AdaNet subnetworks ensemble neural network*

Here the output of the subnetworks is combined to generate one output. It essentially uses the ensemble learning concept, where the final model is composed of simpler ones. This makes the model more complex, but it can also deliver better accuracy.

At each iteration, the algorithm checks a set of candidate networks and evaluates which one improves the ensemble performance (or technically speaking, produces a smaller loss), and then adds that to the ensemble. It is important to note that each candidate network architecture must be provided by the user.

Let's look at few ensemble examples to get an idea of the possibilities.

Figure 5-15 is an ensemble of subnetworks with different complexities. Essentially, the ensemble is composed of increasingly complex neural network subnetworks whose outputs are simply averaged.

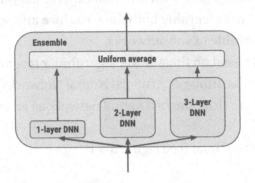

Figure 5-15. *AdaNet subnetwork ensembles with different complexities*

Figure 5-16 is an ensemble learned on top of a shared embedding. This ensembling style is useful when the majority of the model parameters are an embedding of a feature. The individual subnetworks' predictions are combined using a learned linear combination.

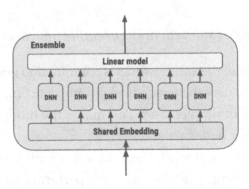

Figure 5-16. *AdaNet ensembles learned from a shared embedding*

Let's now look at the iteration cycle through the lens of Python objects. This helps us with learning and using the framework (see Figure 5-17).

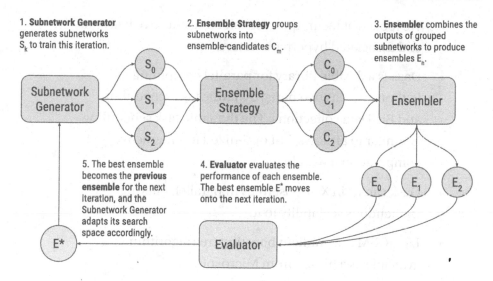

Figure 5-17. *AdaNet ensemble generation process (Source: AdaNet documentation)*

- **Subnetwork Generator** and **Subnetwork** are defined in the `adanet.subnetwork` package.

- **Ensemble Strategy**, **Ensembler**, and **Ensemble** are defined in the `adanet.ensemble` package.

As an exercise, we encourage you to run the examples hosted on Google Colab (`https://github.com/tensorflow/adanet`). The notebooks are well annotated and provide ready-to-use boilerplate code to use in your ML tasks.

Summary

Let's do a quick recap of what was covered in this chapter.

- sklearn doesn't have built-in module stacking. ML-Ensemble (a.k.a. mlens) is an open source library that simplifies experimenting with ensembling. The API style is similar to Keras, and stacking can be built easily by layering base learners and metalearners.

- We looked at techniques for selecting effective learners and associated hyperparameters.

- Dask is a flexible library for parallel computing in Python and has two parts: dynamic task scheduling and Big Data collections. The dynamic task scheduling is similar to airflows, but optimized for interactive computational workloads.

- Dask can train XGBoost trees in parallel, offering tremendous scalability to it.

- LightGBM is a gradient boosting tree algorithm available as a library from Microsoft.

- Histogram-based methods, treating missing values, and gradient-based one-side sampling and exclusive feature bundling has helped LightGBM perform better than XGBoost.

- AdaNet is a lightweight TensorFlow-based framework for automatically learning high-quality models with minimal expert intervention. It is an algorithm for iteratively learning both the **structure** and **weight** of a neural network as an **ensemble of subnetworks**.

As you can see, libraries offer flexibility, reusability, and speed for building ensembles. In Chapter 6, you learn the art of effectively applying ensembles to real-world situations.

CHAPTER 6

Tips and Best Practices

In order to fully extract the power of ensembling, you need to learn the art of effectively applying it to real-world situations.

If you have heard of the 80/20 rule for data wrangling in machine learning, then you know that a vast amount of time is spent beyond searching and optimizing models. By the end of this chapter, you will have a good collection of reusable solutions to integrate ensembles into your real-world ML workflows.

The following are your learning goals for this chapter.

- Feature selection using a random forest model. It should not come as a surprise that feature selection and feature relevance benefits from the performance and interpretation of machine learning algorithms.

- Feature transformations with ensembles of trees.

- Building a preprocessing pipeline for a random forest regressor.

- Isolation forests, an efficient algorithm for outlier detection, especially in high-dimensional datasets.

- Scaling ensembles with Dask.

© Alok Kumar and Mayank Jain 2020
A. Kumar and M. Jain, *Ensemble Learning for AI Developers*,
https://doi.org/10.1007/978-1-4842-5940-5_6

Feature Selection Using Random Forests

It is quite common to have hundreds of features available for your ML task, but they may not all play equal roles, and some may play no role at all. Features that have very low or no importance can be safely removed from the features list. This feature pruning (or the selection of important ones) offers three benefits.

- It reduces the computational cost and time of training a model.

- It makes trained model interpretation easier.

- It reduces overfitting by reducing the variance.

Random forests (an ensemble of decision trees) are popular for feature selection. You can intuitively measure a feature's importance by looking at how much the tree nodes that use that feature improve purity on average (across all trees in the forest). Thus, by pruning trees below a particular node, you can create a subset of the most important features.

Fortunately, scikit-learn computes each feature's importance score automatically after training and then scales the results so that the sum of all the feature importances is equal to 1. You can access the result using the feature_importances_ variable. Let's go through the code in Listing 6-1. We skipped the imports for brevity.

Listing 6-1. Computing feature importance in scikit-learn

```
iris = datasets.load_iris() # -1
feature_list = iris.feature_names # -2
print(feature_list)
['sepal length (cm)',
 'sepal width (cm)',
 'petal length (cm)',
 'petal width (cm)']
```

```python
X = iris.data # -3

y = iris.target # -4

X_train, X_test, y_train, y_test = train_test_split(X, y,
test_size=0.33, random_state=42) # -5

rf_clf = RandomForestClassifier(n_estimators=10000, random_
state=42, n_jobs=-1) # -6

rf_clf.fit(X_train, y_train) # -7

for name, score in zip(iris["feature_names"], rf_clf.feature_
importances_):
    print(name, score) # -8

sepal length (cm) 0.09906957842524829

sepal width (cm) 0.038804978907157164

petal length (cm) 0.4152569088750478

petal width (cm) 0.4468685337925464

y_pred = clf.predict(X_test) # -9

accuracy_score(y_test, y_pred) # -10

0.9333333333333333

sfm = SelectFromModel(clf, threshold=0.15) # - 11

sfm.fit(X_train, y_train) # -12

X_important_train = sfm.transform(X_train) # -13

X_important_test = sfm.transform(X_test)

rf_clf_important = RandomForestClassifier(n_estimators=500,
random_state=0, n_jobs=-1) # -14

rf_clf_important.fit(X_important_train, y_train)
```

```
y_important_pred = rf_clf_important.predict(X_important_test) # - 15
```

```
accuracy_score(y_test, y_important_pred)
```

```
0.9166666666666666
```

Let's unpack the code to better understand it.

1. Use the iris dataset. It is available along with the sklearn library, and hence, you don't need to download the data separately.

2. Retrieve the feature list by using the dataset.feature_names property.

3. Extract the features from the dataset.

4. Extract the target from the dataset.

5. Split the data into train and test by using the train_test_split method available in sklearn.

6. Initialize RandomForestClassifier with 10K estimators.

7. Call the fit method.

8. Once the training is complete, use the feature_importances_ variable to check the importance score. It seems that in the iris dataset, petal length and width are more important.

9. Predict the test set.

10. Calculate the accuracy score. We recalculate the accuracy after feature selection.

11. Create a selector object that will use a random forest classifier to identify features that have an importance of more than 0.15.

12. Train the selector.

13. Create a new dataset by transforming the data containing the important features only.

14. Initialize a new `RandomForestClassifier` with 500 estimators.

15. Fit the classifier and predict the newly created `X_important_test`.

Even though accuracy dropped when trained with only important features, the dataset size reduced by 50%. There was a 2% drop in accuracy with a 50% drop in number of features—that's not bad!

Even if you use other techniques for feature selection, random forests are very handy for quickly understanding which features actually matter in initial experiments.

Feature Transformations with Ensembles of Trees

Decision tree forests are quite popular for **classification** and **regression** tasks because of their robust nature and support of high dimensions, and they are easy to explain. They can also be used to extract embeddings.

An **embedding** is a projection of an input into another more convenient representation space. Embeddings make it easier to do machine learning on large input, like sparse vectors representing words. Ideally, an embedding captures some of the semantics of the input by placing semantically similar input close together in the embedding space. An embedding can be learned and reused across models. If it reminds you of word2Vec and gloVec, then you have a good intuition about embeddings!

In the context of a tree ensemble, a forest embedding represents a feature space using a random forest.

The encoding can be learned in a supervised or unsupervised manner.

- In a **supervised** case, you use the forest tree structures trained for the classification or regression problem to extract the embeddings.

- In an **unsupervised** case, there are no target variables; each tree of the forest builds splits at random.

So how is the embedding generated? It is surprisingly straightforward.

1. Train a random tree forest for your classification or regression problem.

2. Pass the sample through each tree and note which leaf node it ends up in.

3. Mark the leaf node as 1, in which the decision tree places the sample; otherwise, mark it as 0.

4. Concatenate the vectors together.

Visually, the process can be imagined as shown in Figure 6-1.

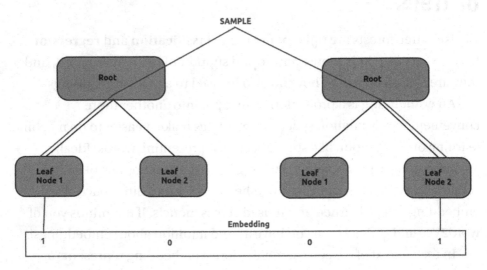

Figure 6-1. *Embedding process. Source: David Vassallo, February 26, 2020.*

Let's go through an example to better understand this. In the tree in shown in Figure 6-2, there are three features: income, age, and credit rating (CR). There are 10 terminal nodes (yes/no). The final embedding looks something like [0, 0, 0, 0, 0, 0, 0, 0, 0, 1]. You end up with an embedding that has a large number of dimensions given that a forest can have hundreds of similar trees. Remember that we built this high-dimensional data from three-dimensional features only.

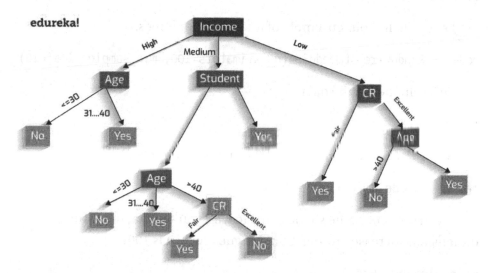

Figure 6-2. *Source: Upasana Priyadarshiny, https://dzone.com/ articles/how-to-create-a-perfect-decision-tree*

You may wonder about the benefit of high dimensionality. In high-dimensional spaces, linear classifiers often achieve excellent accuracy.

Fortunately, we don't need to write the logic; sklearn already offers it with **sklearn.ensemble.RandomTreesEmbedding.** RandomTreesEmbedding is an unsupervised transformation of a dataset to a high-dimensional sparse representation. A datapoint is coded according to which leaf on each tree it is sorted into. Using one-hot encoding of the leaves leads to a binary coding with as many ones as there are trees in the forest. Let's check the concept in code.

We will use the dummy classification dataset available in sklearn.

```
X, y = make_classification(n_samples=80000)
```

Let's check the shape of the data. The second dimension is the number of features here.

```
print(X.shape)
(80000, 20)
```

Let's initialize our ensemble of totally random trees.

```
model = RandomTreesEmbedding(n_estimators=100, min_samples_leaf=10)
```

Fit the model on the data.

```
model.fit(X, y)
```

Apply trees in the forest to X to return the leaf indices.

```
leaves = model.apply(X)
```

If you now check the shape of the leaves, you see that the feature dimensions increased to 100. Can you guess why it is 100?

```
print(leaves.shape)
(80000, 100)
```

Now, we apply a sparse one-hot encoding to the leaves.

```
M = OneHotEncoder().fit_transform(leaves)
```

The encoding is ready for classification or to be used by other machine learning algorithms.

Let's go through another code example (see Listing 6-2) to compare the unsupervised embeddings with supervised embeddings. To do the comparison, we will transform features into a higher dimensional, sparse space, and then train a linear model on these features.

Listing 6-2. Inspired from scikit-learn Documentation

```
n_estimator = 100

X, y = make_classification(n_samples=80000) # - 1

X_train, X_test, y_train, y_test = train_test_split(X, y,
test_size=0.5)  # - 2

X_train, X_train_lr, y_train, y_train_lr = train_test_split
(X_train, y_train, test_size=0.5) # -3

rt = RandomTreesEmbedding(max_depth=3, n_estimators=n_
estimator,random_state=0) # -4

rt_lm = LogisticRegression(max_iter=1000) # -5

pipeline = make_pipeline(rt, rt_lm) # 6

pipeline.fit(X_train, y_train)

y_pred_rt = pipeline.predict_proba(X_test)[:, 1]

fpr_rt_lm, tpr_rt_lm, _ = roc_curve(y_test, y_pred_rt) #-7
```

Let's unpack the code.

1. Use a dummy classification dataset available in sklearn.

2. Split the data in train and test. We are using train_ test_split from sklearn only.

3. Train the ensemble of trees on a different subset of the training data than the linear regression model to avoid overfitting.

4. Initialize the tree ensembles.

5. Initialize the logistic regression.

6. Create a pipeline connecting the random tree ensemble to the logistic regression.

7. Train the pipeline, calculate the probabilities estimates on the test set, and then calculate the roc_curve value.

To reiterate, the preceding code is for an unsupervised transformation using totally random trees. Next, we will do supervised transformation using a random forest.

```
rf = RandomForestClassifier(max_depth=3, n_estimators=
n_estimator)

rf_enc = OneHotEncoder()

rf_lm = LogisticRegression(max_iter=1000)

rf.fit(X_train, y_train) # -8

rf_enc.fit(rf.apply(X_train)) # -9

rf_lm.fit(rf_enc.transform(rf.apply(X_train_lr)), y_train_lr)
# -10

y_pred_rf_lm = rf_lm.predict_proba(rf_enc.transform(rf.apply
(X_test)))[:, 1] #-11

fpr_rf_lm, tpr_rf_lm, _ = roc_curve(y_test, y_pred_rf_lm) # -12
```

Let's unpack the code.

1. Train a random forest classifier on the data.

2. Apply the tree in the forest to the data (X_train), and then fit the one-hot encoder on the returned leaf indices.

3. Apply the tree in the forest to the logistic regression data subset, transform it using the earlier trained one-hot encoder, and fit the logistic regression model on top of it.

4. Calculate the probabilities estimates on the test set, and then calculate the roc_curve value.

To reiterate, the preceding code was for a supervised transformation using a random forest. Next, we will do supervised transformation using gradient boosted trees.

The code is almost identical to what we did for a random forest.

grd = GradientBoostingClassifier(n_estimators=n_estimator)

```
grd_enc = OneHotEncoder()

grd_lm = LogisticRegression(max_iter=1000)

grd.fit(X_train, y_train)

grd_enc.fit(grd.apply(X_train)[:, :, 0])

grd_lm.fit(grd_enc.transform(grd.apply(X_train_lr)[:, :, 0]),
y_train_lr)

y_pred_grd_lm = grd_lm.predict_proba(grd_enc.transform
(grd.apply(X_test)[:, :, 0]))[:, 1]

fpr_grd_lm, tpr_grd_lm, _ = roc_curve(y_test, y_pred_grd_lm)
```

For comparison, let's calculate the roc_curve for gradient boosted and random forest models.

```
y_pred_grd = grd.predict_proba(X_test)[:, 1]
fpr_grd, tpr_grd, _ = roc_curve(y_test, y_pred_grd)

y_pred_rf = rf.predict_proba(X_test)[:, 1]
fpr_rf, tpr_rf, _ = roc_curve(y_test, y_pred_rf)
```

Let's plot the roc_curve for all the options.

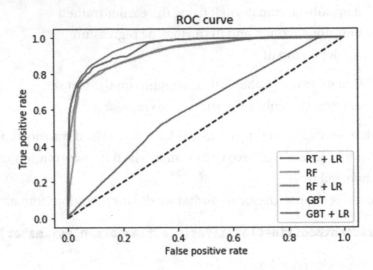

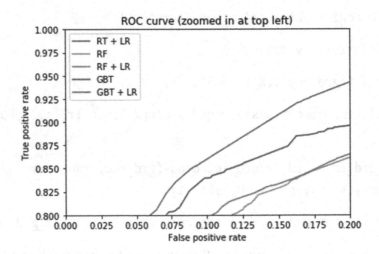

It is evident that ensemble-based embedding is an excellent preprocessing step for linear classification tasks.

Building a Preprocessing Pipeline for a Random Forest Classifier

In an ideal world, the data is perfect. Unfortunately, we are not living in a perfect world. Before ensembling the models, data requires preprocessing. Thanks to sklearn, there are robust building blocks to effectively set up the preprocessing pipeline.

We will build a preprocessing pipeline combined with prediction using **sklearn.pipeline.Pipeline** and a random forest classification model. We will use the titanic dataset to build a binary classifier for survivors.

The classifier will be trained with the following numeric features.

```
# - age: float.
# - fare: float.
```

It will be trained with the following categorical features.

```
# - embarked: categories encoded as strings {'C', 'S', 'Q'}.
# - sex: categories encoded as strings {'female', 'male'}.
# - pclass: ordinal integers {1, 2, 3}.
```

Let's fetch the dataset using fetch_openML, which downloads the data from the openml.org repository. openml.org is a public repository for machine learning data and experiments; it allows anyone to upload open datasets. Since sklearn 0.22.2, you can specify the as_frame parameter to return the data as a dataframe. This is quite useful for exploration and experimentation.

```
np.random.seed(0)
X, y = fetch_openml("titanic", version=1, as_frame=True,
return_X_y=True)
```

Let's explore the dataset. The info() method is useful for getting a quick description of the data; particularly the total number of rows, each attribute's type, and the number of non-null values.

```
X.info()

<class 'pandas.core.frame.DataFrame'>
RangeIndex: 1309 entries, 0 to 1308
Data columns (total 13 columns):
pclass        1309 non-null float64
name          1309 non-null object
sex           1309 non-null category
age           1046 non-null float64
sibsp         1309 non-null float64
parch         1309 non-null float64
ticket        1309 non-null object
fare          1308 non-null float64
cabin         295 non-null object
embarked      1307 non-null category
boat          486 non-null object
body          121 non-null float64
home.dest     745 non-null object
```

Note that while there are 1309 instances, the age column only has 1046 values indicating missing values. We need to handle the missing values in our pipeline.

Let's explore the categorical fields. You can use the value_counts method for it. This method tells you the total number of categories and entries per category.

```
X['pclass'].value_counts()
3.0    709
1.0    323
2.0    277
```

```
X['sex'].value_counts()
male       843
female     466

X['embarked'].value_counts()
S    914
C    270
Q    123
```

Let's create the preprocessing pipelines for both numeric and categorical data.

All the missing age values will be replaced with a median strategy (i.e., the median of the Age column). You could easily guess other potential strategies.

- If mean, then replace the missing values using the mean along each column. This can only be used with numeric data.

- If median, then replace the missing values using the median along each column. This can only be used with numeric data.

- If most_frequent, then replace the missing values using the most frequent value along each column. This can be used with strings or numeric data.

- If constant, then replace the missing values with fill_value. This can be used with strings or numeric data.

StandardScaler standardizes features by removing the mean and scaling to unit variance.

The standard score of a sample, x, is calculated as

$$z = (x - u) / s$$

where *u* is the mean of the training samples or zero if `with_mean=False`, and *s* is the standard deviation of the training samples or one if `with_std=False`.

The **standardization** of datasets is a common requirement for many machine learning estimators. They might behave badly if the individual features do not resemble standard normally distributed data (e.g., Gaussian with a 0 mean and unit variance). Note that **random** forests and gradient boosting are not sensitive to the magnitude of variables. So, **standardization** is not **needed** before fitting these kinds of models. They have been added here for the sake of completion.

```
numeric_features = ['age', 'fare']
numeric_transformer = Pipeline(steps=[
    ('imputer', SimpleImputer(strategy='median')),
    ('scaler', StandardScaler())])
```

`OneHotEncoder` encodes categorical features as a one-hot numeric array. The input to this transformer should be array-like integers or strings that denote the values taken on by categorical (discrete) features.

```
categorical_features = ['embarked', 'sex', 'pclass']
categorical_transformer = Pipeline(steps=[
    ('imputer', SimpleImputer(strategy='constant', fill_
value='missing')),
    ('onehot', OneHotEncoder(handle_unknown='ignore'))])
```

So far, we have created the categorical and numerical columns transformer separately. However, it would be more convenient to have a single transformer that can handle all columns and applies the appropriate transformations to each column automatically. In version 0.20, scikit-learn introduced **ColumnTransformer**, which offers this feature. It also works great with Pandas dataframes.

```
from sklearn.compose import ColumnTransformer
preprocessor = ColumnTransformer(
    transformers=[
        ('num', numeric_transformer, numeric_features),
        ('cat', categorical_transformer, categorical_
        features)])
```

First, you need to import the ColumnTransformer class. Next, you initialize ColumnTransformer with the list of numerical and categorical column names. The constructor requires a list of tuples, where each tuple contains a name, a transformer, and a list of names (or indices) of columns that the transformer should be applied to.

In our case, numeric_features should be transformed using numeric_ transformer, and categorical_features should be transformed using categorical_transformer.

Our pipeline is almost ready. We finally need to add the classifier, which in our case is a random forest.

```
rnd_clf = RandomForestClassifier(n_estimators=255,n_jobs=-1)
pipeline = Pipeline(steps=[('preprocessor', preprocessor),
                           ('classifier', rnd_clf)])
```

Would it be a surprise if we split our data into training and testing before feeding it to the pipeline?

```
X_train, X_test, y_train, y_test = train_test_split(X, y,
test_size=0.2)
```

Finally, the moment has arrived to fit the pipeline on the data.

```
pipeline.fit(X_train, y_train)
print("model score: %.3f" % clf.score(X_test, y_test))
```

Did you notice that our random forest was initialized with 255 estimators? Where did this number come from? Well, we used grid search to find the best parameters. In fact, for real-world problems, a pipeline optimized with search (grid search, random search, etc.) is the norm. Let's add grid search to our pipeline.

First, we need to import GridSearchCV. Next, we need to define the search space of all the parameters that we are interested in.

```
from sklearn.model_selection import GridSearchCV
# Number of trees in random forest
n_estimators = [int(x) for x in np.linspace(start = 100, stop =
300, num = 10)]
# Number of features to consider at every split
max_features = ['auto', 'sqrt']
# Maximum number of levels in tree
max_depth = [int(x) for x in np.linspace(10, 110, num = 11)]
max_depth.append(None)
# Minimum number of samples required to split a node
min_samples_split = [2, 5, 10]
# Minimum number of samples required at each leaf node
min_samples_leaf = [1, 2, 4]
# Method of selecting samples for training each tree
bootstrap = [True, False]
```

Next, we prepare the parameter grid. Note that are we using the transformer name along with a double underscore to map the parameter to a specific transformer.

```
grid = {'classifier__n_estimators': n_estimators,
            'classifier__max_features': max_features,
            'classifier__max_depth': max_depth,
          'classifier__min_samples_split': min_samples_split,
            'classifier__min_samples_leaf': min_samples_leaf,
            'classifier__bootstrap': bootstrap}
```

The following is what our parameters search space looks like.

```
pprint(grid)
```

```
{'classifier__bootstrap': [True, False],
 'classifier__max_depth': [10, 20, 30, 40, 50, 60, 70, 80, 90,
   100, 110, None],
 'classifier__max_features': ['auto', 'sqrt'],
 'classifier__min_samples_leaf': [1, 2, 4],
 'classifier__min_samples_split': [2, 5, 10],
 'classifier__n_estimators': [100, 122, 144, 166, 188, 211,
   233, 255, 277, 300]}
```

Let's initialize the GridSearchCV.

```
search = GridSearchCV(estimator = pipeline,param_grid = grid,
cv = 3, verbose=2, n_jobs = -1)
```

It's time to fit the grid search model.

```
search.fit(X_train, y_train)
```

You can check the best parameters value via the best_params_ attribute.

```
print(search.best_params_)
{'classifier__bootstrap': True, 'classifier__max_depth': 10,
'classifier__max_features': 'auto', 'classifier__min_samples_
leaf': 2, 'classifier__min_samples_split': 10, 'classifier__n_
estimators': 255}
```

The pipeline and grid search are not ensemble-specific, but knowing how to use them effectively with ensembles leads to very accurate ensembles.

Isolation Forest for Outlier Detection

An **isolation forest** is an efficient algorithm for outlier detection, especially in high-dimensional datasets. The algorithm builds a random forest by picking a random feature and a random threshold value (between the min and max values) to split the dataset. The dataset splitting continues until all instances end up isolated from other instances. Outliers are less frequent than regular observations and usually have different values. On average (across all the decision trees), they tend to get isolated in fewer steps than normal instances. Let's take a look at this visually.

In Figure 6-3, the red points denote the anomalous points.

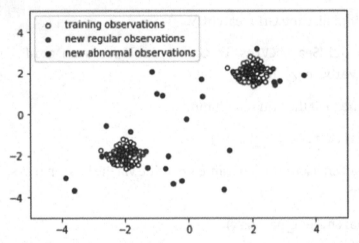

Figure 6-3. *A dummy dataset containing regular and abnormal observations*

As you can see, normal points are clustered, whereas anomalous points are further away from other points. Thus, while randomly partitioning the domain space, the anomaly is detected in a smaller number of partitions than a normal point. A smaller number of partitions indicate a shorter distance from the root node (i.e., fewer edges traversed to reach the terminal node from the root node). The number of splittings (or partitions) required to isolate a sample is equivalent to the path length from the root node to the terminating node.

Random partitioning produces noticeably shorter paths for anomalies. Hence, when a forest of random trees collectively produces shorter path lengths for particular samples, they are highly likely to be anomalies. Figures 6-4 and 6-5 illustrate this point.

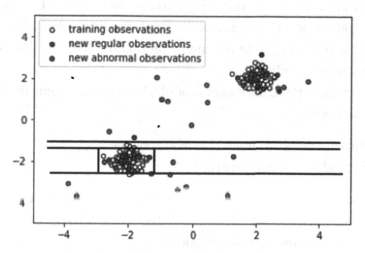

Figure 6-4. *Isolating a normal point*

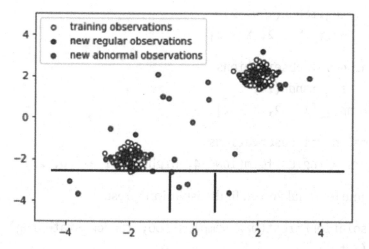

Figure 6-5. *Isolating an anomalous point*

Whether a point is a normal or an anomalous is indicated by the path length. An isolation forest algorithm returns the anomaly score of each sample.

To interpret the score as a probability, it helps to represent the score between 0 and 1. For example, if we get an anomaly score of 0.7, then we interpret that the point has a probability of 70% to be an anomalous point.

Now that you have an idea of how isolation forests work, let's use the implementation in code.

Let's first import the necessary module. We removed some of the imports for brevity.

```
from sklearn.ensemble import IsolationForest
rng = np.random.RandomState(42)
```

Let's generate the data. Regular novel observations for train and test are generated from a standard normal distribution, whereas the outliers are generated from uniform distribution.

```
# Train data
X = 0.3 * rng.randn(100, 2)
X_train = np.r_[X + 2, X - 2]

# Regular novel observations
X = 0.3 * rng.randn(20, 2)
X_test = np.r_[X + 2, X - 2]

# Abnormal novel observations
X_outliers = rng.uniform(low=-4, high=4, size=(20, 2))
```

It is time to initialize and fit the isolation forest.

```
clf = IsolationForest(max_samples=100, random_state=rng)
clf.fit(X_train)
```

With the model trained, it's time to generate the predictions.

```
y_pred_train = clf.predict(X_train)
y_pred_test = clf.predict(X_test)
y_pred_outliers = clf.predict(X_outliers)
```

Let's plot and visualize (see Figure 6-6) the predictions of the isolation forest.

```
xx, yy = np.meshgrid(np.linspace(-5, 5, 50),
np.linspace(-5, 5, 50))
Z = clf.decision_function(np.c_[xx.ravel(), yy.ravel()])
Z = Z.reshape(xx.shape)
plt.title("IsolationForest")
plt.contourf(xx, yy, Z, cmap=plt.cm.Blues_r)
b1 = plt.scatter(X_train[:, 0], X_train[:, 1],
                 c='white',s=20, edgecolor='k')
b2 = plt.scatter(X_test[:, 0], X_test[:, 1],
                 c='green',s=20, edgecolor='k')
c = plt.scatter(X_outliers[:, 0], X_outliers[:, 1],
                 c='red',s=20, edgecolor='k')
plt.axis('tight')
plt.xlim((-5, 5))
plt.ylim((-5, 5))
plt.legend([b1, b2, c],
           ["training observations",
            "new regular observations", "new abnormal
            observations"], loc="upper left")
plt.show()
```

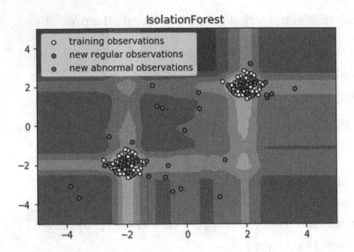

Figure 6-6. *Isolation forest predictions*

An isolation forest is quite unique when compared with other outlier detection algorithms. It introduces the use of isolation as a more effective and efficient means to detect anomalies than the commonly used basic distance and density measures. It builds a good performing model with a small number of trees using small subsamples of fixed size, regardless of the size of a dataset.

Scaling Ensembles with Dask

There are two distinct scaling problems that you might face while ensembling. The scaling strategy depends on which problem you're facing.

- **Large models**: Although the data fits in RAM, you may have a large ensemble of many models.

- **Large datasets**: The data is larger than the RAM, and sampling isn't an option.

Dask can help scale ensembles.

- For large models, use `dask_ml.joblib` and your favorite scikit-learn estimator.

- For large datasets, use `dask_ml` estimators.

To scale an ensemble pipeline, you need to think beyond large models and datasets. Recall the pipeline and grid search. Dask has modules for preprocessing and parameter space search.

Preprocessing

dask_ml.preprocessing contains some scikit-learn style transformers that can be used in pipelines to perform various data transformations as part of the model fitting process. These transformers work well on Dask collections (dask.array, dask.dataframe), NumPy arrays, or Pandas dataframes. Again, to reiterate, why use Dask for preprocessing? Well, it fits and transforms in parallel.

Table 6-1 lists some of the transformers that are (mostly) drop-in replacements for their scikit-learn counterparts.

Table 6-1. *Dasks drop-in transformer replacements for scikit-learn counterparts*

Transformer	Description
MinMaxScaler([feature_range, copy])	Transforms features by scaling each feature to a given range.
QuantileTransformer([n_quantiles, …])	Transforms features using quantile information.
RobustScaler([with_centering, with_scaling, …])	Scales features using statistics that are robust to outliers.
StandardScaler([copy, with_mean, with_std])	Standardizes features by removing the mean and scaling to unit variance.
LabelEncoder([use_categorical])	Encodes labels with a value between 0 and n_classes-1.

There are two important things to keep in mind while using dask_ml.preprocessing.

- They operate on Dask collections in parallel.

- .transform returns dask.array or dask.dataframe when the input is a Dask collection.

Table 6-2 lists a few other Dask transformers that are helpful for converting non numeric data into numeric data.

Table 6-2. *Dask transformers to convert numeric data into numeric data*

Transformer	Description
Categorizer([categories, columns])	Transforms DataFrame columns to a categorical dtype.
DummyEncoder([columns, drop_first])	Dummy (one-hot) encode categorical columns.
OrdinalEncoder([columns])	Ordinal (integer) encode categorical columns.

These transformers are useful as a preprocessing step in a pipeline where you start with heterogeneous data (a mix of numeric and non-numeric), but the estimator requires all numeric data.

Let's go through a toy pipeline to check the transformer in code. Our pipeline will

- Categorize the text data

- Dummy encode the categorical data

- Fit a RandomForestClassifier

Let's import the necessary libraries.

```
from dask_ml.preprocessing import Categorizer, DummyEncoder
from sklearn.linear_model import RandomForestClassifier
```

```
from sklearn.pipeline import make_pipeline
import pandas as pd
import dask.dataframe as dd
```

Initialize the Dask dataframe from the Pandas dataframe.

```
df = pd.DataFrame({"A": [1, 2, 1, 2], "B": ["a", "b", "c", "c"]})
X = dd.from_pandas(df, npartitions=2)
y = dd.from_pandas(pd.Series([0, 1, 1, 0]), npartitions=2)
```

Build and fit the pipeline.

```
pipe = make_pipeline(Categorizer(),DummyEncoder(),RandomForestC
lassifier())
pipe.fit(X, y)
```

The code is self-explanatory if you know about pipelines in general, but the following is a quick explanation for the sake of completion.

Categorizer converts a subset of the columns in X to a categorical dtype. By default, it converts all the object dtype columns.

DummyEncoder dummy (or one-hot) encodes the dataset. This replaces a categorical column with multiple columns, where the values are either 0 or 1.

We encourage you to read sklearn.preprocessing documentation (https://scikit-learn.org/stable/modules/preprocessing.html) to learn more about available transformers.

Hyperparameter Search

There are two kinds of hyperparameter optimization estimators in Dask-ML. The appropriate one to use depends on the size of your dataset and whether the underlying estimator implements the partial_fit method.

If the dataset is relatively small or the underlying estimator doesn't implement partial_fit, dask_ml.model_selection.GridSearchCV or dask_ml.model_selection.RandomizedSearchCV can be used. These are drop-in replacements for their scikit-learn counterparts; they should offer better performance and handling of Dask arrays and dataframes.

Drop-in Replacement for scikit-learn

dask_ml.model_selection. GridSearchCV	Exhaustive search over specified parameter values for an estimator.
dask_ml.model_selection. RandomizedSearchCV	Randomized search on hyperparameters.

Incremental Hyperparameter Optimization

The second category of hyperparameter optimization uses *incremental* hyperparameter optimization. These should be used when your full dataset doesn't fit in the memory of a single machine.

In Dask, dask_ml.model_selection.IncrementalSearchCV is the class that handles this. This class incrementally searches for hyperparameters on models that support partial_fit.

Broadly speaking, incremental optimization starts with a batch of models (underlying estimators and hyperparameter combinations) and repeatedly calls the underlying estimator's partial_fit method with batches of data.

Read the documentation to learn more about it.

Distributed Ensemble Fitting

The remaining pieces are ensemble fitting and predictions. To reiterate, we are exploring how Dask is used for ensemble training and prediction.

Let's consider a case in which we use the scikit-learn estimator, but the dataset is larger than the memory. Dask ensures that not all data is loaded at once.

Let's import the necessary libraries.

```
from sklearn import datasets
from sklearn.ensemble import GradientBoostingClassifier
import dask_ml.datasets
from dask_ml.wrappers import ParallelPostFit
```

The only new imports are dask_ml datasets and ParallelPostFit.

dask_m.datasets is equivalent to sklearn.datasets. We use it to create a large toy dataset.

ParallelPostFit is a metaestimator for parallel prediction and transformation. Think of it as a distributed score function (in sklearn). It is important to note that this class is not appropriate for parallel or distributed *training* on large datasets. For that, use Dask Incremental; it provides distributed (but sequential) training.

Let's make a small, 1000-sample training dataset and fit normally.

```
X, y = datasets.make_classification(n_samples=1000, random_
state=0)
clf = ParallelPostFit(estimator=GradientBoostingClassifier(),
                        scoring='accuracy')
clf.fit(X, y)
```

Let's build a bigger toy dataset.

```
X_big, y_big = dask_ml.datasets.make_classification(n_
samples=100000, random_state=0)
```

Prediction on the new Dask input is no different than what you do in sklearn. The highlight here is that the classifier works on prediction datasets that are larger than the memory.

```
clf.predict(X_big)
```

	Array	Chunk		
Bytes	800.00 kB	200 B		1
Shape	(100000,)	(25,)	100000	
Count	8000 Tasks	4000 Chunks		
Type	int64	numpy.ndarray		

Let's build a voting classifier now. Recall that a Voting classifier model combines multiple models (i.e., subestimators) into a single model, which is (ideally) stronger than any of the individual models alone.

But why use Dask? Dask provides the software to train individual subestimators on different machines in a cluster. This enables users to train more models in parallel than is possible on a single machine. Let's explore the Voting classifier with Dask in code.

Let's import the necessary modules.

```
from sklearn.ensemble import VotingClassifier
from sklearn.linear_model import SGDClassifier
from sklearn.ensemble import RandomForestClassifier
from sklearn.svm import SVC
import sklearn.datasets
X, y = sklearn.datasets.make_classification(n_samples=1_000,
n_features=20)
```

```
classifiers = [
    ('sgd', SGDClassifier(max_iter=1000)),
    ('rf', RandomForestClassifier()),
    ('svc', SVC(gamma='auto')),
]
clf = VotingClassifier(classifiers, n_jobs=-1)
```

You saw all of this code in earlier chapters.

Let's initialize the dask-distributed cluster. Again, we discussed this in Chapter 5.

```
import joblib
from distributed import Client
client = Client()
with joblib.parallel_backend("dask"):
    clf.fit(X, y)
```

This familiar code is the benefit and beauty of scaling ensembles with Dask. The key takeaway is to remember the scalable options available for the preprocessing, training, and prediction tasks of your ensemble pipeline.

Summary

Let's do a quick recap of what was covered in this chapter.

- Random forests are very handy in learning which features matter. You can use the feature_ importances_ variable of the estimator.

- Forest embedding represents a feature space using a random forest. Embeddings give higher dimensionality to features, which help linear classifiers achieve excellent accuracy.

- sklearn offers a good toolset for building an ensembles preprocessing pipeline. `sklearn.pipeline` can build a transformer pipeline.

- sklearn `ColumnTransformer` provides a consistent way to connect pipelines.

- An isolation forest is an efficient algorithm for outlier detection, especially in highly dimensional datasets. It isolates observations by randomly selecting a feature and then randomly selecting a split value between the maximum and minimum values of the selected feature.

- `dask_ml.preprocessing` contains some scikit-learn style transformers that can be used in pipelines to perform various data transformations as part of the model-fitting process.

- There are two kinds of hyperparameter optimization estimators in Dask-ML. The appropriate one to use depends on the size of your dataset and whether the underlying estimator implements the `partial_fit` method.

- **Dask ParallelPostFit** is a metaestimator for parallel prediction and transformation.

- Dask provides the software to train individual subestimators on different machines in a cluster. This enables users to train more models in parallel than would have been possible on a single machine.

Thank You

Well, we have reached the end of the book, and we would like to sincerely thank you for reading it until the end. We truly hope that you will be able to effectively apply ensembling techniques in your projects.

If there are any errors, please do not hesitate to send feedback. Feel free to contact us via Apress or Twitter at @aloksaan and @mayank10j.

The best way to get maximum value from the book is to do one thing: practice. Try running all the codes snippets in the book. Find a project where you can try ensembles.

Our greatest hope is that this book inspires you to add ensembles as a regular tool in your machine learning skills toolkit and to push the boundaries of ensembles. Happy learning.

Index

A

AdaBoost
    classified data, 50
    classifier, 52
    correctly classified
        observations, 50
    scikit-learn, 52
    voting of n learners, 51
AduNet
    ensemble generation process, 95
    ensembles learned, shared
        embedding, 94
    lightweight TensorFlow-based
        framework, 93
    subnetwork ensembles with
        different complexities, 94
    subnetworks ensemble neural
        network, 93
Averaging, 35–37

B

Bagging
    aggregating, 22
    bootstrapping, 22
    classifier, 24
    ensemble technique, 21
    mixing training data, 3
    primitives, 22–24
    sampling with replacement, 21
    scikit-learn, 24
    training step, 22
Balanced tree, 87
Boosting
    AdaBoost, 50–52
    definition, 5, 50
    gradient, 52–55
    learning process, 49
    XGBoost, 55–57
Bootstrap aggregating, *see* Bagging
Bootstrapping, 22

C

Classifier, 50
Cross-validation, 25

D

Dask
    architecture, 74
    parallelize custom algorithms,
        dask.delayed interface, 76
    delayed function, 77
    2D arrays tasks graph, 79

© Alok Kumar and Mayank Jain 2020
A. Kumar and M. Jain, *Ensemble Learning for AI Developers*,
https://doi.org/10.1007/978-1-4842-5940-5

E

Printed in the United States
By Bookmasters